STORIES FROM A YELLOW PAD

COLLECTION OF SHORT STORIES

Romana Capek-Habekovic

Copyright © *Romana Capek-Habekovic*, 2025

All Rights Reserved

This book is subject to the condition that no part of this book is to be reproduced, transmitted in any form or means, electronic or mechanical, stored in a retrieval system, photocopied, recorded, scanned, or otherwise. Any of these actions require the proper written permission of the author.

Table of Contents

One 1
   The American Story 2
   The Piano Teacher 7

Two 32
   Peter 33
   Elisa 41
   Marina Vlady 63
   Sara's Birthday 67
   The Letter to Mila 73
   Little Miss Pink 74
   All grown-up 75

Three 80
   Homes 81
   Balconies 85
   Old Neighborhoods 95
   Plumbing by Jim 102
   Sprinklers by Tom 109

Four 113
   The Desert 114
   My Smith-Corona 123
   Feathered Fear 128
   Last Cigarette 137

Five 146
   The Lake Effect 147
   Pride Month 153

Six 163
    The Pumpkin Field 164
    The Squid and the Whale 173
    The Wedding 179
    The Letter 187
    Seduction Pronto Lang Style 199

ONE

The American Story

The evening sneaked up on me, and when P.G. parked her red convertible at the end of our driveway, it took me by surprise. I thought that she was supposed to come the following week. She was on my mind that afternoon, and I was looking forward to our meeting since we had not seen each other for a while. In the meantime, our lives evolved, especially hers after a recent divorce, and mine in a smaller measure. It did not matter that one of us got the wrong date; I was just happy watching her walking toward the house. I waited for her at the open entrance. We greeted and hugged each other, and I wanted to ask her where her children were, when she explained that Lisa, the oldest of her four kids, stayed home to babysit her brothers.

"I didn't feel like bringing them along because I would not be able to talk freely. I wanted to bring Marty, but he was too shy to come. Perhaps he'll join us the next time."

Why would she ever bring Marty? I thought. I have nothing in common with a retired salesperson from *Sears*. He was her second husband and about twenty years her senior.

Before entering the house, she beamed at her convertible.

"You didn't see it yet. I just got it. I love it! It's great!"

"Yeah, looks super. I bet that the May breeze feels wonderful?"

"I didn't have it in May. Next May I'll feel it."

P.G. looked fantastic. She was one of those people whose outer appearance reflects her mental and emotional harmony. Her honey-colored locks of hair cascaded down to her shoulders and framed her make-up free freckled face and dimpled cheeks. She wore dentures at seventeen because she was afraid of dentists; consequently, a dentist had to extract all her teeth because of irreparable cavities and gum infections.

"I hated dentists, so I lost them," she once told me.

"Come in the living room," I invited her. "What can I give you? Cafe?"

"No, do you have a beer?"

"I do. I'll join you."

She faced me sitting in the orange velvet upholstered chair with her right leg resting on the knee of her left in a way men do it. Such a relaxed position leaves a gap between legs that suits men because they wear pants, but women in the same sitting position wearing dresses or skirts would reveal their underwear. I never saw P.G. in a dress or a skirt, probably because she wanted to feel free to choose where and how she was going to sit. That evening she wore jeans, tucked in her high-heeled boots and cuddly pink top. There was nothing refined in her manners and speech, and yet she looked regal to me because she felt so comfortable in her own skin.

"What about you? What is happening?" she asked me.

"Oh, not much new. Life goes on as usual, working, driving kids around, and taking care of the house. You know the same old crap."

"I really wanted to bring Marty; he is great. If not for him, I would have already gone nuts. Don frequently skips the alimony for the boys. I make $4.50 an hour at the Hamburger Place, work there eight-hour shifts, and deliver pizza four hours every night."

"What do you do at the Hamburger Place?"

"I make patties, and occasionally I advertise the food in front of the restaurant by wearing a giant hamburger costume. That's how I met Marty. He introduced himself by telling me that he liked how the cheese hung out of my buns." She grinned remembering that sentence.

"What an existence being a full-time hamburger! But it puts the food on the table."

I looked at P.G. and just loved hearing her talk void of self-pity and dignified in her selfless care for her family. Her outlook on life was both positive and realistic at the same time. I envied her mental steadiness and the zest for life she succeeded in keeping in spite of any hardship she was enduring.

"God, Marty is incredible! Lisa hates him because he is so old. I don't care. I fell in love with him when he first touched my hand. Oh Jesus, I shivered all over. I would have stayed with him in his house that afternoon, but the kids were due home from school. I would have stayed."

P.G. was all aglow talking about Marty and their eating at different restaurants, about his divorce, and about his jealousy when Don visits their boys.

"Oh, yeah, he is great! I wouldn't trade him for anybody younger."

I believed her. She was sipping her beer slowly, thoroughly enjoying it. To her, life had a full flavor. She took what was in front of her without interjecting her past into it or projecting her future. P.G. was not shallow, not at all; she had just figured out the right way to live. By talking to her, I learned about existential basics, about things that matter and those that should be left alone or pushed aside.

"God, we are so different, and yet at that moment I felt so close to her," I thought. By comparison with P.G., I saw myself as a shadow of an existence.

"P.G., I envy you. I really do."

"Come on, for what?" My question surprised her.

"I have had nothing but troubles since I can remember. You know what" –she switched the subject – "I don't like that guy Mike. I had mentioned him to you. He spends too much time with Lisa and drinks a lot. She is too young for him. Lisa thinks that I hate him, and I do. He has no business being near her. I have to tell him that. What the hell, it is my house, and I don't want that jerk to put moves on my daughter."

P.G.'s anger made her freckled face red, but her eyes remained mild. She was not capable of hating somebody. Her sudden burst of ire was a result of her constant worry for her daughter's well-being.

"Are you taking any vacation this year?" She shifted our conversation in my direction because she did not want to continue talking about herself and her family.

"Maybe, but it is still up the air. We have not decided yet. It all depends on when Dean will be able to take time off."

Our exchanges jumped from one subject to the other. P.G. talked fast, often finishing her sentences with a laugh. I loved that about her because by doing so she created lightness in the air.

"I like your jeans and the top. Where did you get it?" I asked her.

"At Meijer's. Marty hates it when I wear tight jeans and blouses that reveal too much. He always tells me to unbutton just a few buttons down from the collar because he does not want men to stare at my boobs. I like it when he is jealous." She winked.

I glanced at our new piano behind P.G., an elegant addition to our living room. All the furnishing in it was carefully selected and expensive. Dean and I enjoyed living surrounded by nice things.

"Where did you buy these blue leather chairs? I didn't see them the last time I was here." She picked up on my thoughts.

"At Hudson's Warehouse sale, I paid them only $300 apiece."

"You must be kidding me! I could furnish my whole living room for that kind of money." Her reaction was just a statement, not a judgment, on my spending or envy.

I wanted to ask her more about Marty. Her family thought that she had left Don to be with Marty, but this was not true. Years living with an alcoholic who refused any help took a toll on their relationship. She stopped loving Don. This was the real reason behind their divorce and the most honest one.

Suddenly I felt emotionally spent. I thought about last night that was again one of those hit and run events. Nowadays I call my sex life a screw. We do it several times a week, after the eleven o'clock news and before the beginning of the late-night movie. I leave the family room at 11:30 to take off my makeup and brush my teeth. I turn off the light, put on my nightgown, and lay on the far right of our king size bed. Soon after, my husband comes out of the dark hallway into the bedroom, drops his clothes by the bedside, and slides next to me. The room is silent, our dialogue stopped at the dinner table, if there was one, and we begin to screw. It is a lonely trip to a climax because the letdown starts with my husband's resolute lifting of my nightgown and his mechanical touching of my breast. I lose track of time, but he makes sure not to miss the beginning of the movie. He gets out of bed, puts his clothes on, and exits the bedroom. There are no embraces and passionate kisses before the first dream, the love evaporated into darkness.

Life is not predictable; it is multidimensional and changes like a chameleon. Why do I feel captured in only one of its forms? The truth eludes me. I am sure that P.G. has an answer for me, but I am not ready to hear it, not yet.

"I have to go, that jerk Mike is probably still in my house, and Lisa doesn't know how to get rid of him. Call me when you are free. Next time I'll bring Marty. I want you to meet him. He is a great guy!"

"P.G., it's been great seeing you!"

I hugged her soft, warm body, and her tender squeeze made me forget last night.

"P.G., you are such a great person!"

"Oh, come on, I am just a walking hamburger, remember?!"

I watched her briskly walking to her red car and thought how lucky I am to have her in my life.

The Piano Teacher

"Sometimes life seems to move in circles and land us at the same spot where we once were," Anna Clamp thought as she watched her daughter Mila picking up the car keys with her usual motion of an unprovoked rush. With her purse in hand and a map with the Detroit area code, she headed out the door to visit her old piano teacher, Mrs. Blake. Anna admired Mila's devotion to her old friends and acquaintances and the effort she put into staying in touch with all of them even after her move to LA years ago, a case in point being Mrs. Blake.

It was one of those subzero December days in Michigan covered in snow that seldom melts before March. Christmas was fast approaching, and Anna was still looking for meaningful gifts. This shopping frenzy never fazed Mila. Being always well organized, she would bring all her presents for the family and friends that she had bought in LA before her trip back home in a suitcase. She would wrap them upon her arrival and stack them under the nine-foot-tall Christmas tree in the living room. That day she put aside meeting her friends and, instead, decided to spend a few hours with Mrs. Blake.

Anna stayed at home alone browsing through her recipes for holiday desserts that she wanted to bake before Christmas Eve. She was looking forward to smelling the aroma of the spiced rum she added to several of her cookie recipes and to watching the slow melting of the semisweet chocolate in a small pan. She would turn the kitchen into a pastry shop with bags of flour and sugar, pounds of butter, grinded nuts, baking pans in different sizes, and cooling racks. This chaotic scene permeated with different olfactory sensations created the pre-Christmas festive atmosphere that Anna enjoyed.

She seldom thought about Mrs. Blake, but Mila's visit to her reminded her of the weekly piano lessons she would give to both of her children, first to Joe when he was a young boy and several years later to Mila. Joe hated those lessons because Mrs. Blake was not able to develop a friendly student-teacher rapport with him. She was strict and demanded hours of practice before their meeting. The lesson would begin with repetitions of scales, corrections of hand positions, and proceeded with playing from pages with notes that she had assigned to practice a week earlier. Joe did not like to practice, and he ignored Mrs. Blake's stern looks and admonitions. Furthermore, he loathed recitals at the end of the school year during which all Mrs. Blake's students were supposed to play a short piano composition in front of their parents and siblings. Those recitals were meant to demonstrate the progress they had made throughout the year. Joe did not care if his technique improved. He played his piece mechanically, happy to have it over quickly.

Anna's insistence on Joe's musical instruction stemmed from her own desire to have learned how to play the piano when she was his age. She had briefly attended a music school. The first lessons focused on students listening to different musical sounds and illustrating images that those created in their minds. Anna was able to draw what the teacher expected to see, but when the lessons required playing those sounds on the piano, she had to quit music school. Her parents could not afford even a used piano; thus, she was unable to practice. She thought that not having learned to play an instrument and lacking a thorough musical education deprived her of fully enjoying and understanding classical music. She did not want Joe to feel the same one day. In spite of it, she decided that it was pointless to have her son continue with piano lessons because he hated them so much that he even stopped saying "hello" and "by" to Mrs. Blake.

Mila, six years younger than Joe, replaced him on the piano bench. Mrs. Blake was in Anna's house again once a week. This time the relationship between her and Mila was completely different. It resembled the one between a grandmother and a granddaughter. Mrs. Blake became more of a surrogate grandmother than a teacher. Mila's maternal and paternal grandmothers lived in another state and would see her and Joe throughout summer vacations, but they did not show much interest in their grandchildren. Anna's mother preferred preparing meals instead of spending time with them while they stayed in her house, and her mother-in-law would choose days and times when they could visit her. Consequently, neither of the two grandmothers got to know Mila and Joe. They failed to see anything wrong with their relationship with them, but the children felt ignored. When Mrs. Blake came along, Mila took full advantage of her attention.

The piano that Joe played on was an old, antique white upright of an unknown make that the previous owner of the house had left in the living room. Anna did not like the color of it and painted it light brown. She also had it tuned. The piano tuner was a short man, of slight build with a crown of curly blond hair and a deep voice. He restored the piano keys, replaced a few lost ones, and made it play. He continued to tune this old piano, as well as the new one Anna bought for Mila, after seeing how much her daughter loved to practice and enjoyed her lessons with Mrs. Blake. The new piano was a shiny black Yamaha upright. The old one Anna donated to a nearby Catholic church.

Mila's lessons followed the same pedagogical method, as did those of Joe. She did not mind the initial technical part of it because Mrs. Blake praised every correct note she pressed and gently coached her to redress the wrong ones. After one hour of teaching, Mrs. Blake would sit at the piano and play different compositions while Mila would put her pink tutu on and her ballet slippers and dance around the living room giggling. The teacher would look at her twirling and laugh aloud in her husky voice. Sometimes the two of them would play a game instead. Anna would hear them raising their voices signaling that when one of them had won.

Despite being only in her early sixties and having just a few students, Mrs. Blake would sometimes confuse the day when she was supposed to give Mila a lesson. She would arrive on the wrong day when Mila had her ballet class, and not having found anybody home, she had to return to her apartment. One time she showed up on Saturday when Mila's birthday party was in full swing. She was embarrassed and wanted to leave immediately, but Anna insisted that she stay and celebrate with other guests. She declined the offer of a slice of cake because of her gluten allergies but enjoyed a glass of wine.

Mrs. Blake's mind was sharp otherwise, and Anna sometimes wondered if she would intentionally come prior to the scheduled day because she wanted to be paid earlier. Anna thought that her income from social security and the piano lessons should have sufficed for covering her expenses.

When Mrs. Blake came the following week, she brought a gift for Mila – a book of easy piano compositions that she would be able to play. Mila would always get a small Christmas present from her as well. Anna saved a glass, pink angel that her daughter forgot to take with her when she had moved to LA. The delicate figurine still stands on the top of the black upright next to the piano lamp.

When Anna and her family moved into a new house, Mrs. Blake continued to give Mila lessons until she graduated from high school. Her last recital took place in the semi-empty living room of that new home. Students and their parents sat on an old sofa covered in a fabric with large blue and orange flowers and on folding metal and upholstered chairs. Anna was afraid that the wood floor would reflect sound, and the high ceiling would create an echo, thus causing a cavernous acoustic. Fortunately, the piano sounded fine. Mrs. Blake arrived dressed in her everyday clothes, but changed into a loud, flowery blouse and beige lightweight pants. By putting on her festive attire, she showed her appreciation for her students and their families. She headed straight to an empty chair next to the piano and briefly greeted the audience. After she sat down, she began to take out of her canvas bag a pile of music books from which her students would play. In the meantime, Anna distributed the program that Mrs. Blake gave to her earlier. Everyone noticed the teacher's nervousness, her sweat-covered face, and a panicky look. Anna was afraid that she might have a stroke, but Mrs. Blake calmed down as soon as her first pupil began to play.

Each of the fifteen students played his or her song, and the recital was over in less than two hours. The quality of playing varied from very bad to acceptable, but the parents did not blame the teacher for it. Instead, most of them wished not to have pushed their unmotivated children to learn how to play piano. Their reason for doing it was probably the same as Anna's, who insisted on a musical education for her children. At the end of the recital, she thanked the teacher and students for their diligent work and the parents for their support. Mila gave Mrs. Blake a bouquet of flowers, and she seemed pleased. Anna expected her to become at least a bit emotional because it was the last time that she would be in their home, but she understood why the teacher considered a sufficient expression of gratitude just to be a simple "thank you!" She remembered Mrs. Blake's description of her growing up in Australia as the oldest daughter in a family with four other children in which showing emotions meant being weak. Her mother died when she was a teenager, and she helped her father take care of the house and her siblings. She would cook, clean, and wash everyone's clothes. To eliminate the chaos at home, her authoritarian father imposed strict rules that his family had to obey. He was especially hard on her, but she forgave him because, she said in her thick Australian accent, "Daddy bought the piano just for me, and I loved him for it, if not for anything else." In her rare free time, she taught herself how to play the piano.

Anna prepared a simple reception following the recital for her guests to mingle, get to know each other, and talk to Mrs. Blake. As she observed the cheerful crowd filling up their plates with finger food and their glasses with fruit punch, she realized that one part of her life was over and that soon she and her husband would be empty nesters. At that moment, she did not see Mrs. Blake only as a piano teacher. Instead, she saw her as an integral part of her family, weaved into their life narrative, an unforgettable presence. She was the last one to leave after the reception. Anna hugged her heavy-set body, wished her well, and many more students in the future. Mila embraced her as well but seemed eager to see her gone because her leaving meant that Mila's new life as a student had begun. Young people bear departures much easier than adults because they see far into the future, imagining it rosy and without thorns, while the older we get, our past and memories of it tend to enhance our feelings about the present. We perceive the future in terms of immediacy. Anna shut the door after Mrs. Blake, and sadness overwhelmed her. She made a cup of coffee and sat at the kitchen counter looking outside at the wetland behind their house and began to cry. Mila was already in her bedroom talking to her friends on the phone and giggling, making plans for the evening outing.

The screechy opening of the garage door signaled that Mila had returned from visiting Mrs. Blake. She hung up her coat and took off her boots before entering the kitchen. Anna and her husband were watching TV stretched out on a long, comfortable sofa.

"How was your visit? How is Mrs. Blake doing?"

"Well, mama, let me tell you what is going on with her," Mila looked horrified, eager to describe what she saw at the piano teacher's house.

"The house looks terrible. One of the two bedrooms has a half-burned roof and most of the walls. Cardboard covers both windows. Mrs. Blake told me that her daughter Cibola burned it down."

"Oh my God, this is horrible. Is Cibola living with her?"

Anna hated that name. "How could anyone name a child Cibola? It sounds like a disease."

"She lives in the basement, but I didn't go downstairs. Thankfully, she was not home. Mrs. Blake told me that she was in prison because she had been caught selling drugs on the street."

"I understand now why Mrs. Blake was sometimes eager to get paid earlier. She must have supported Cibola using her social security check and the money she was earning from the piano lessons. How does she look?"

"She moves around either pushing a walker or maneuvering her electric wheelchair. She has lost almost all her teeth. The house is a mess, and it reeks."

"How is her mental state?"

"She is cheerful, wanted to know all about me and you guys. We also talked about a time when I had visited her in Texas."

"I remember that you went to see her during one of your spring breaks. If I recall correctly, she lived there with her older daughter for a while. I forgot her name. She told me that the reason why she returned to Michigan was Cibola, who needed her help."

"I was glad to have visited her because she seemed happy to have her daughter and grandchildren around. She gave up teaching, though. She told me that she wanted her daughter to bury her in Texas next to her husband because she owns a grave there. Mama, I think that we need to do something to help her now."

"You are right. I am going to call her and arrange a meeting in her house. I'll see what I can do."

Mila flew back to LA the day before New Year's Eve. She liked to celebrate it with her friends. It took Anna several days to get used to her being gone. She missed her happy personality, her unrestrained laugh, her zest for life, and her bare feet peeping under her fluffy pajama bottoms in the morning. Mila's preference for dumping her clothes on the floor instead of hanging them in her walk-in closet, her scattering shoes all over the house, and her leaving behind dirty glasses and plates on whichever surface was closer didn't bother her. Anna began to teach at the beginning of January. The work routine helped her shed the blues after Mila's departure, and she decided to visit Mrs. Blake.

The teacher was surprised by Anna's phone call and even more amazed when she told her about her plan to see her at the end of January. While slowly driving on the snow-covered roads, she recalled conversations she had with Mrs. Blake throughout the many years that they had known each other. One time the teacher told her about her marriage to a much older bachelor, a successful businessman in an Australian lumber company. She had married him to escape her tyrannical father and her unhappy domestic life. The man, Mr. Blake, promised her that after they got married, they would move to the United States. She accepted his proposal without hesitating. Anna imagined her being very attractive as a young woman with curly red hair, blue eyes, and porcelain white skin, characteristics attributed to those of Irish descent. He told her that they would not have children because a childhood disease left him sterile. Well, she had become pregnant already in the first year of their marriage, but he doubted that the child was his. He took a fertility test that proved his earlier diagnosis wrong. When Mrs. Blake would describe their doctor's interpretation of the test result, she would always end it with an exclamation sentence and a hearty laugh. "There were millions of them, millions!" she said, referring to her husband's sperm count.

Their second daughter, Cibola, was born in the United States. The family lived in Texas. Mrs. Blake began to give piano lessons on her old piano that her husband shipped from Australia, and he spent long hours at work. She did not talk much about their marriage, but one time she mentioned to Anna that when Cibola was a teenager, her husband began to molest her. At first, she only had doubts, but when her daughter's behavior radically changed, she was sure. Her beautiful, vivacious, bright child became taciturn, moody, rebellious, and difficult to handle. She blamed that incestuous trauma for Cibola's later drug addiction. Mrs. Blake felt at fault for not defending her daughter, as she should have. Anna dared to ask her why she let the abuse continue.

"I was scared to leave him, to be left alone in a new country with two small children and no money. He was also violent and used to hit me for no reason, but his was not the first beating I have suffered. My daddy used to beat me as well."

"Did you go to the police and report him?"

"No, I was too scared that he would hurt the children and kill me."

After one of her husband's violent outbursts, she filed for a divorce and fled to Michigan. He remained in Texas without any further contact either with her or with their daughters. He reconciled with the older one a few years before his death.

When Anna first met Mrs. Blake, she lived in a tall red-brick residence for independent seniors. She had a one-bedroom apartment there and a parking place for her Oldsmobile. The well-kept building had a large weekly mowed lawn, and the planters in front of the main entrance were full of floral arrangements.

Cibola lived elsewhere. She became an alcoholic and a drug addict. When she was not in prison, she bounced from job to job. Anna was not certain when Mrs. Blake decided to buy a house and move in with her daughter. This was a bad decision because she did not know how an addicted person behaves and what he or she is capable of doing. Cibola began to steal money from her and valuables that she could sell. One time, she even stole her car, but Mrs. Blake blamed thieves for it since her house was not in a safe neighborhood. The next-door neighbor disputed her account of the theft and told her that he saw Cibola driving away in the Oldsmobile and returning in a taxi. Mrs. Blake ended up reporting her to the police, but when she was supposed to testify in court against her daughter, she withdrew her original statement, and Cibola was back home. Anna thought that a few months of incarceration would help Cibola get off of drugs and enable her to function in society. Mrs. Blake did not see it that way.

"I think that the guilt for not protecting Cibola from her father clouded her judgment," Anna concluded.

She reached Mrs. Blake's Street, lined on both sides with small bungalow-style homes built in the fifties for Ford's assembly line workers. They consisted of two bedrooms, a small living room and a kitchen, one bathroom, and a basement. They had fenced yards, above ground pools with slides, and swing sets. If a household had two vehicles, one would stay on a short driveway by the house and the other on the street. Most of the cars and trucks looked dilapidated because of their rusted bodies caused by the exposure to elements and unrepaired collisions. Anna spotted the teacher's house on the right side of the street, parked in front of it, and rang the bell. In a few minutes, Mrs. Blake appeared at the door leaning on her walker. She smiled broadly and hugged her. She offered Anna a seat in the kitchen and asked her if she would like some tea.

"I would love a cup of tea. It will warm me up. It's so cold today," Anna replied. Mrs. Blake put the kettle on the stove to heat the water.

At that moment, Cibola quickly passed by Anna, grabbed her green worn-out jacket out of a small coat closet at the entrance, and with her head down, never looking at Anna, asked:

"Hi, are you parked on the street?"

"Yes, I parked on the street."

"Mom, I need your car keys. I have to run an errand."

"Ok, here they are. When are you going to be back?"

"I don't know."

Anna glanced at Cibola and saw a tall, slender woman, with an unruly mop of curly red hair and a freckled face. The physical resemblance to her mother was uncanny. Her edgy movements and eagerness to leave the house looked like she urgently needed something to calm her down. This was an adrenaline rush that if not satisfied would make her explode in rage.

While chatting with Mrs. Blake, Anna looked around. The tiny kitchen was in disarray: dirty dishes piled up in the sink and on counters, the walls were full of smudges, the floor was sticky from spilled food and different liquids, and different papers cluttered the small kitchen table. The window blind had a broken cord, and remained shut, after Mrs. Blake unsuccessfully tried to pull it up. Anna noticed gallons of milk in front of the side door. Mrs. Blake explained that they had to keep them outside because the refrigerator was not working properly. The milk would often freeze because Cibola would leave it too long in below-zero temperatures. She had a cat and fed it with the milk that she poured in a small bowl and left inside of the door. The teacher hated the cat because its hair flew everywhere, and its muddy paws dragged throughout the house.

The kettle whistled, and Mrs. Blake asked Anna to get herself a mug and a tea bag from a tin container in one of the kitchen cabinets. When Anna opened the cabinet, she regretted her decision to have tea. The grimy inside of it was repulsive. She filled up the mug with hot water, dunked the tea bag in it, and never touched it again. Mrs. Blake wanted to show her the house, and first she opened the door to the charred bedroom. The acrid smell of smoke was still there. Cardboards and sheets of a plastic tarp covered the windows and the gaping hole in the roof. The walls and the floor seemed damp from the large amount of water the firefighters had to use to extinguish flames. Mila's description of the room was not exaggerated.

"I woke up to the smell of something burning," Mrs. Blake explained.

"Cibola was asleep in the basement, and I immediately called 911. We both could have been killed."

"What caused the fire?"

"Cibola decorated the room with strings of colorful lights. There were too many, and a fuse caught fire."

"I bet that this was Cibola's version of the incident that she gave to the firefighters," Anna thought. She was probably heating up heroin and ignited piles of papers scattered across the floor, Anna concluded.

"Mrs. Blake, this room needs to be fixed. You are losing a lot of heat through windows and the half caved-in ceiling. Did you call your insurance company?"

"Yes, I did, but they still did not send an appraiser to see the damage."

"Give me the number of your insurance company and your policy number. I will give them a call," Anna offered to help knowing that Cibola was not going to take care of it because she was the one who needed the most help.

Mrs. Blake's bedroom was also a mess, and it reeked of urine because she used the potty during the night so as not to have to walk to the bathroom. Her queen size bed was untidy, and its headboard was leaning against half-stripped wallpaper with pink roses on it. The nightstand crowded with different bottles of her medicines stood next to it. Some of her clothes lay on a single chair in the room, the others hung in the closet with only one door; the other one was missing. Anna recognized several of her blouses and pants that she used to wear when she came for the piano lessons. The living room did not look any better than the rest of the house. The sofa had stains on it and Cibola's cat scratched the fabric with its paws. The window that overlooked the street had most of the vertical blinds' slats missing. Anna took a quick look at the bathroom because its door was open. She saw a rusty faucet and a sink full of soap scum and hair.

The last place to see was the basement. Mrs. Blake said that Cibola did not allow anybody to come downstairs. She herself was not able to because the stairs were steep, and the railing was missing. Since Cibola was not in the house, Anna decided to take a look. The scene in front of her resembled an urban slum dwelling that she only saw in the movies. The basement was dim with only one light centered on the ceiling. Some of Cibola's clothes were hanging on a clothes rack; the rest of them she kept on and in carton boxes spread throughout the basement. She slept in a twin bed on soiled sheets half covered with a stained dark green blanket. Her drug paraphernalia was on a chair next to the bed. Her worn-out shoes and boots lay all over the cement floor. Two garbage cans stood in one corner as well as empty wine and whiskey bottles along with beer cans Cibola stashed in the other. The basement was full of run-down pieces of furniture she probably bought in garage sales. Everything she owned was in that basement, a fitting symbol for the person she was. Anna remained speechless for having witnessed how deeply one can fall and just continue to exist. She had never looked in the face of such a tragedy of human despair and continued debouched living. Anna realized that Cibola had hit bottom and was dragging her mother with her.

When Anna climbed up the stairs, she saw Mrs. Blake waiting for her to describe what she saw in the basement. She paused for a few seconds, carefully choosing her words.

"Mrs. Blake, I think that you have to come to some kind of agreement with your daughter regarding her stay with you. She should pay rent and contribute for food."

"I already told her, but she says that she will move out soon and move in with her boyfriend."

"This is good. Well, I will call your insurance company and see how much they will give you to fix the fire damage, but I think that there are other things in the house that need work. For example: paint the entire house, build a ramp from the sidewalk to the entrance to enable you to use the wheelchair, and repair the bathroom which is in bad shape. How does this sound to you?"

Mrs. Blake's face became animated. She smiled and said that she would love to have her house in order.

"I'll let you know when I hear from the insurance company, and then we can plan what to do first. Agreed?"

"Great! Great!" Mrs. Blake clapped excitedly.

As soon as Anna returned home, she called Mila to describe her visit to Mrs. Blake. She told her about her plans to help the teacher get back on her feet and begin to enjoy her retirement. Mila was happy to hear that because she knew that her mother was always good at putting things in order. She was indeed a perfect person to create a livable environment for Mrs. Blake. Anna was an efficient organizer to the point of being obsessive about it. Mila remembered that in her parents' home, everything had its designated place, and each item had a label on it. Her mother even color-coded her work-related papers, important documents, contracts with repair people and home-improvement companies. She even sorted photographs by themes and dates. For example, she had separate albums for each trip abroad, family vacations, and gatherings with friends. At work, she was just as devoted to order and organization. She never procrastinated, and her colleagues could always count on her to finish their task if they were late doing it.

Throughout growing up, Anna not only perfected her organizational skills, but she also learned how to run a household, not because she wanted to but because her mother demanded it of her. She taught Anna how to iron when she was a preschooler and how to start dinner when she was in the first grade. She also taught her how to mend her father's socks by placing the heel part of them on a round mushroom-like wooden mold that would stretch the heel and expose the hole in it. Anna also helped with a thorough cleaning of their apartment before Easter and Christmas: furniture had to be polished, parquet floors waxed, rugs cleaned with water and vinegar, windows and curtains washed, and freshly starched doilies placed on all surfaces suitable for them. After those cleanings, her mother always complained about being exhausted, and yet the results made her happy. At that time, Anna did not mind doing her share because she felt like a grown-up. She continued to do the same type of scrubbing and polishing in the first twenty years of her marriage until she finally realized that it was a waste of her energy and time.

Anna decided that setting up an appointment with Mrs. Blake's insurance company must be a priority. A fire damage evaluator came the following week, and he explained to Mrs. Blake that her insurance policy only covered fire and water damage in the burned bedroom, but no other repairs such as plumbing and electrical. The house needed many more repairs for which she did not have money. Anna figured out that she could involve her neighbors and several friends who often volunteered in different organizations in the whole project. Chris and Debby, her church-going neighbors, used to build homes in Ukraine and Russia as members of a volunteer group sponsored by the House of Lord Presbyterian Church. They were also helping their fellow worshippers who needed either material or moral assistance. The couple agreed to see Mrs. Blake's house. Anna hoped that after they witnessed the conditions in which she lived, they could find a few good Samaritans with repairperson skills in their church who would do some of the work.

Debby was the first to visit Mrs. Blake. Being a pianist herself, she was especially shocked to see the filthy and dilapidated home that was not a place for any musician to live in. Mrs. Blake told her that she had to leave her piano in the basement of one of her former student's parents because she could not find anyone to transport it to the house. They did her a favor by keeping it while she was in the process of moving out of her apartment. The parents thought that she would pick it up in a few weeks, and when that did not happen, they became eager to get rid of it. They asked her several times to move the piano to her house because they wanted to finish their basement.

"As soon as the house is fixed, I will arrange its transport," Anna said to Debby.

"I am sure that she misses playing it," Debby replied convinced that neither she nor Mrs. Blake could bear life without music.

Chris came a few days later. Anna walked him through all the rooms, and at the end of the tour, he promised to ask some of his church friends to donate their time to do some of the work on the house.

"Anna, this is a massive project. I'll try to help you in any way I can."

Unfortunately, his friends were all busy volunteering elsewhere.

Debby told Anna that she would help her clean the basement the following Saturday. Mrs. Blake was grateful that they came, and she put the kettle on the stove to have tea ready for them when they would take a break. They both wore their oldest clothes and put on rubber gloves. As soon as they descended into the basement, they saw Cibola looking for something on her bed. She saw them, and visibly irritated asked:

"What are you doing here?'

"Hi, Cibola. This is my friend Debby. We would like to help you clean the basement."

"I don't want you to touch my stuff. Get out of here!" she screamed.

Debby was afraid and insisted that they leave immediately. Since Anna was also uncomfortable, they went upstairs and explained what happened to Mrs. Blake. She was not surprised and said that she would talk to Cibola about it.

While driving home, Anna realized that she was not going to be able to fix the house as long as Cibola still lived there. She explained that to Mrs. Blake, and she asked her to tell her daughter to move out as soon as possible. This must have made Cibola mad because the next time Anna came, the teacher had a large blue bruise on her right arm and a scratch on her right cheek. When Anna asked her what had happened, she told her that she had lost her balance and fallen on the kitchen table, but Anna doubted her explanation. She was certain that Cibola either pushed her mother or hit her.

"Is Cibola going to move out?'

"Yes, in two weeks, she assured me."

Cibola did move out after two weeks had lapsed, and she took just her clothes with her, leaving everything else behind. The next-door neighbor was happy that she was gone because of all the shady characters that she would bring to the house and do drugs with. They would also blast loud music until the wee hours that would frequently wake up his two toddlers. The man also worked two jobs and needed his sleep. He asked her several times to tone down the volume, but she ignored him and shut the door in his face.

Anna had to change her original plan of cleaning the basement with Debby's help. After the last encounter with Cibola, Debby withdrew her offer. Anna thought of another neighbor who once had told her she knew many people downtown who did this type of work for a fee. He gave her several phone numbers to call, but she got only one answer.

"Yes, we can do that," a female voice replied to Anna's inquiry.

"When would you like us to come?"

"As soon as possible."

The crew of three men and one woman came the next day. They worked fast and in an organized manner. It was obvious that they had done a similar clean up many times before. In several hours, they filled two large garbage cans with empty bottles, discarded fast food containers, broken plates, and unworkable umbrellas. The container they set in front of the house was also full of unusable furniture, moldy rugs, and empty boxes. They washed and disinfected the floor with bleach and stacked items that remained in the basement neatly against the walls.

Anna stopped by after work to see what the crew had done. While standing in the middle of a clean, orderly basement, she noticed on one wall facing the back yard a wet spot and a crack across it. She went outside to inspect it and saw a large oak tree with its roots exposed stretching all the way to the house. She figured out that the oak had probably grown into a main pipe that ran the water to the house and caused a leak in the basement. Because of this obstruction in the flow, the pipe released only half of its capacity to the bathroom's sink and shower. This was an additional problem to solve.

"Mrs. Blake, you have a leak in the basement because of the oak tree in your back yard. I have to call a tree company, and then the plumber."

"Ok, whatever you say," Mrs. Blake had reached the point of not wanting to deal with details of the work that was going to be done on her house. She was happy to relinquish decision making to Anna.

Prior to repairing that leak, Anna first had to discuss the financing for it with Mrs. Blake, as well as for other projects. The teacher informed her that she did not have money for a major remodel but that she could ask for a loan from her bank. Anna drove her to the closest branch the same day. The bank manager explained what her options were.

"Mrs. Blake, you qualify for a reverse mortgage because you are over 65."

"What does that mean?"

"We would appraise how much equity you have in your home and based on that we would approve a loan in the amount we can give you.

In return, you would sign your house over to us. You can continue living in it without paying your mortgage any longer. Is this clear?"

The woman talked slowly and loudly seeing an elderly person in a wheelchair in front of her. She stereotyped Mrs. Blake, not knowing that despite her appearance, Mrs. Blake had excellent hearing and a bright mind. Anna was quiet because she wanted Mrs. Blake to make the decision. It was an important one because upon her death, the bank would own her house, thus she could not leave it to her daughters. The teacher listened carefully and thought just for a moment.

"Let's do it! This sounds great! Ha, ha!" She was as thrilled as a kid in a candy shop.

When she received the first check from the loan, she was able to pay the tree company that took care of the roots of the overgrown oak and the plumber who replaced the leaking pipe. She was happy to see a strong stream coming out of the bathroom faucet. While the tree company was still working in the backyard, Anna saw that the grass needed mowing because nobody had done it in years. She asked the next-door neighbor if he would be willing to do it and she would pay for it. Anna was sure that he could use some extra money, but more importantly, he would not have to look at Mrs. Blake's neglected lawn any longer. His was always neat because he mowed it weekly and watered it with a hose during the summer. He carefully planned his backyard and kept it orderly. It had a small vegetable patch in one corner and a swing set in the other. Clay pots filled with annuals circled a patio furnished with a redwood outdoor furniture set probably bought in Sears. He agreed not only to cut grass for Mrs. Baker, but he also threw her rusty aluminum furniture and a broken lawnmower, which were scattered across her backyard, onto the curb. Anna thought of doing a bit of landscaping along the fence. She had several varieties of hosta plants that she could divide in half and plant.

"Hostas will make the backyard more attractive. They grow fast, don't need any special care, have beautiful green leaves, bloom in the late summer, and have a symmetrical shape," Anna suggested to Mrs. Blake, who enthusiastically supported her idea.

Anna continued to keep the teacher informed about the upcoming repairs because she did not want to be the only one making decisions, especially regarding work that would require payment from the loan. The next multiphase project was fixing the charred bedroom. Anna found a drywall specialist to repair the charred drywall and the ceiling, and the insurance company dispatched a roofer. The window company she hired installed two missing windows and replaced a large living room window that leaked and had a deep scratch on one side of the glass. They told her that the more windows they installed, the more the price would go down. This was the main reason she decided to put that new window in the living room. The two men crew worked fast, and the vinyl windows with granite seals were in by the end of the day. The bedroom began to resemble a livable space, but it needed painting.

"Mrs. Blake, what do you think if we paint the entire house?" Anna asked rhetorically.

"Sure, whatever you think we need to do."

"Ok, I'll find a painter. I will stop by Home Depot tomorrow and buy a new faucet for the bathroom sink and check out refrigerators. They sell good brands. The repair of your fridge would cost almost as much as buying a new one. I will also call JCPenney to measure for new blinds in the bedroom and the living room."

Anna was spending more and more time at Mrs. Blake's house, waiting either for different workers to give their estimates or to check on the finished work. At the same time, she suggested that the teacher should take care of her teeth because she had difficulty chewing. Most of her teeth were missing.

"I would love to be able to eat my food without choking. I cannot even talk properly anymore. Unfortunately, I don't have money for a dentist."

"Well, I think it must be something available for people in your position. Let me call the Dental School and see if they could treat you free of charge."

"They would probably assign a dental student to work on my teeth. I am not sure that I want to do it," she hesitated.

"Well, students always work under the supervision of their professors. I am sure of it. You would feel better and look better than you do now," Anna said firmly, trying not to show her annoyance with Mrs. Blake's attitude.

"How would I get to the clinic? I cannot drive that far."

"If the Dental School agrees not to charge you, I'll drive you."

Anna's hunch paid off. The Dental School had a needs-based program for senior citizens, and Mrs. Blake qualified for it. Over the next six months she drove Mrs. Blake thirty miles to her appointments with the assigned dental student. He was a tall, handsome young man who always greeted her with a broad smile and wheeled her into the dental office. Anna would pack lunch for Mrs. Blake because the teacher had to wait until Anna taught her last class in the afternoon and was free to drive her home. Mrs. Blake developed a warm relationship with her dentist in training, and after each visit, she trusted his ability to do a good job more.

The fixing of the house continued. After the painter finished his work, the stench of burning was completely gone. He stripped the wallpaper in Mrs. Blake's bedroom and painted it light pink, as she wanted. The rest of the house had antique white walls. The Flooring and Carpet Company installed vinyl tiles in the kitchen and replaced stained wall-to-wall carpet in both bedrooms and the living room with a sand color remnant. The house was ready for some new furniture. Anna drove Mrs. Blake to a bargain furniture store, and the teacher selected a gray corduroy upholstered sofa with a matching love seat and side table. She also bought a new mattress for her bed and for the queen bed in the other bedroom. That bed frame and the dresser survived the fire because Cibola pushed them for no logical reason into the middle of the room before she moved to the basement. They had some water damage from the hose the firefighters used, but Anna was able to mask it with several coats of furniture polish. Mrs. Blake had two antique table lamps that she liked very much. They had white glass domes on top of a brass stand and needed restoration. Anna took care of it, and the teacher placed one of them on her nightstand and the other one on the side table in the living room.

"I always wanted to get them restored but never got to it. Now I have them. They are gorgeous! Thank you!"

Anna called the parents of Mrs. Blake's former student and asked them to bring her upright piano. They were relieved to be able to get it out of their basement. The teacher was happy to see it in her living room and looked forward to playing it. She gathered her books of musical composition and sorted them on a freestanding short bookshelf next to the piano. One of Anna's friends came to see how the house looked in its present condition. He asked the teacher to play something for him despite Anna having warned him that she was probably rusty and did not want to embarrass herself. He insisted because sensitivity to others was not his strong suit. She wheeled herself to the piano and slid from the wheelchair to the piano bench. She began to play and realized that her technique was gone because arthritis had stiffened her fingers. Anna was upset with the whole scene because her friend, whom Mrs. Blake had met only a couple of times in Anna's house, had humiliated her.

There was one more project on Anna's to-do list - a wooden deck with a ramp in front of the house to enable the teacher to wheel herself to her car parked on the driveway. Since Cibola never brought back her mother's car, Mrs. Blake bought a used Toyota in perfect condition and with low mileage. Anna drove her to the Department of Motor Vehicles to renew her driver's license. Despite having passed the driving test, Anna remained concerned that the teacher's reflexes and week leg muscles could affect her driving. She mentioned that to Mrs. Blake, who assured her that her reflexes were fine and that she would strengthen her leg muscles by using her walker more often instead of the wheelchair. The deck and the ramp built in a couple of days looked sturdy and well designed, and the teacher had the last appointment with her student dentist the following month. Anna's volunteerism was nearing completion, and she felt good about it.

She did not visit Mrs. Blake for four weeks, but she kept in touch by phoning her. When she picked her up for that last dentist's appointment, she noticed that several walls in the kitchen had scuffmarks and the side of one lower cabinet had an indentation as if someone had crashed into it.

"What happened?" she asked the teacher.

"Oh, this is nothing. I was not careful maneuvering my wheelchair, and I hit the cabinet."

On the way-out Anna glanced at the driveway where the Toyota was supposed to be. When she did not see it, she looked at the backyard. There it was – the parked Toyota with its front completely smashed in. Mrs. Blake did not mention anything about it to Anna when they talked on the phone.

"For god's sake Mrs. Blake, what happened?"

"I lost control of the car because I did not brake fast enough, and I ran through the gate. I am sorry. This was such a good little automobile," she calmly answered.

Anna was more upset than the teacher was, and she blamed herself for having encouraged her to buy a car and drive. Her earlier concerns about Mrs. Blake's driving skills were correct, but she had backed down because the teacher was eager to regain her independence.

The dental student was pleased with how the dentures fit in Mrs. Blake's mouth. They not only improved her smile, but they also enabled her to pronounce all her words clearly. Moreover, she was finally able to chew her food, which eliminated her digestion problems. The young man embraced her after having wheeled her to Anna's car. It was a happy scene, and a fitting ending to the yearlong work on improving Mrs. Blake's life.

When Mila flew from LA to celebrate the following Christmas with the family, she visited her old piano teacher. She could not believe how different both she and the house looked.

"Mama, you really saw this whole project through!" she said and hugged Anna.

"Yes, it took all my free time, but I was happy doing it, especially after seeing Mrs. Blake's life improving after each phase of the renovation. She can finally live comfortably in her house."

Anna continued to call Mrs. Blake once a month, and she told her, in case she ever needed help with anything, to give her a call. The winter semester was almost over, and she was looking forward to spending a few months abroad. She planned to leave at the end of June but wanted to visit Mrs. Blake before her trip because during her last call, the teacher sounded unnaturally cheerful.

"Something is going on. She always sounds uplifting but her burst of cheerfulness was over the top," Anna thought.

She called the teacher to tell her that she would like to see her before her departure. Anna announced her visit because she wanted to give her time to get herself ready for their meeting. Appearances were always important to Mrs. Blake. She opened the door and greeted Anna warmly. While they hugged, Anna looked over the teacher's shoulder at the kitchen behind her. It was as messy as when she had seen it for the first time: dirty dishes piled up in the sink, all the counters covered with fast food containers and the dirty glasses, the floor was sticky from spilled drinks, and scuffmarks were on all the walls. As they were entering the kitchen, Mrs. Blake saw Anna's disappointment.

"I am sorry; it is a bit messy in here. I had a cold last week and spent it in bed. I feel better now," She tried to justify the look of her kitchen, but Anna did not believe her.

"How is Cibola? Have you seen her lately?" Anna wanted to hear the truth.

"Oh yes, she stopped by a few times when I was sick, just to drop off groceries." The teacher delayed her answer for a few seconds searching for a credible lie. She did not expect Anna's direct questions.

"Well, I just wanted to see how you are doing. I will be in town at the end of August. I cannot stay because I have an appointment," Anna lied because she wanted to leave immediately, especially after having noticed Cibola's sandals at the landing above the basement stairs.

When she sat in her car, she took one last look at the house and saw several slats missing from vertical blinds in the living room. "Cibola is back," Anna concluded, and at that moment decided not to contact Mrs. Blake ever again. She gave her all to help her and requested only that Cibola move out of the house. I guess this was too much to ask. She understood the teacher's love for her daughter because the mother's love is constant even for a fallen child. She also knew that the guilt for not preventing her husband from molesting Cibola resided deep in her soul, and yet she felt that Mrs. Blake had betrayed her.

"It looks like I put her in a position to choose between Cibola and me. I should have known from the start that I had no right to interfere in the lives of these two women and try to alter the dynamic in their relationship. I always remained an outsider regardless of my altruistic and noble intentions. I considered the piano teacher a part of my family while she saw me first as a source of her income, and later as a good-natured and generous acquaintance," Anna rationalized her feelings because she regretted not recognizing Mrs. Blake's view of their relationship. It took her some time to reverse the course of her thinking:

"Well, whatever happened in the past, is behind me. I had fun working on her house, and that is worth something."

Several years passed. Mila graduated from college and graduate school, and she got married. Anna had an appointment near Mrs. Blake's neighborhood and decided to stop by her house. She wanted to see how the teacher was doing. She buried her grievances, and her hurt was gone. After several knocks on the door, nobody opened it. She turned around and saw the next-door neighbor appearing on his porch.

"Mrs. Blake moved to Dallas a couple of years ago and lives there with her other daughter. She left her cell phone number. If you want it, I can give it to you. Cibola stayed in the house."

"Thank you for telling me. I did not know it. No, I don't need her phone number."

A few months later, Anna received a large envelope with the sender's Dallas address. Inside was a letter in which Mrs. Blake asked her if she would be willing to be the executor of her will. She named her daughters as beneficiaries. She wanted her savings, investments in bonds and stocks, and jewelry to be distributed equally between the two of them. The total value of her assets was small. Anna waited for a while before she declined the teacher's request. Knowing Cibola's history, she was certain that she would contest that will and would demand a larger share of it. Anna did not want to partake in any messy family disputes.

Mila's Yamaha piano, which Mrs. Blake had selected for her decades ago, stays in her spacious, sunny living room in LA now. She plays it still, reading the music from the books that Mrs. Blake gave to her through many years of piano lessons. It seems as if the piano teacher had never left her. The memory of her lives on because she touched and enriched Anna's family life in so many ways that she will be forever grateful for the gift of Mrs. Blake.

TWO

Peter

Donald hung up the phone in the kitchen and said matter-of-factly, "Peter Hermann went down with his plane in the Gulf of Mexico." Claire looked at him puzzled, not being able to react for a few seconds. She was waiting for more details, but experience had taught her that if she wanted to learn more about anything that Donald crammed into a single sentence, she had to follow up with her own inquiry.

"When did it happen?" Claire asked in disbelief, looking at Donald's unemotional face.

"I guess a week ago. George didn't know for sure."

George kept in touch with Donald and Peter after their college graduation. Donald, on the other hand, was happy to hear from George but seldom called him, and they both lost track of Peter after he had moved to New Orleans.

"To where did he fly?" Claire insisted on more details.

"From New Orleans to Florida," Donald answered, laconically turning his back to Claire and heading toward the family room. For him their conversation was over.

He stretched out on the sofa, lit his cigarette, and turned on the television. He watched three reruns daily without getting bored. Claire sometimes joined him while correcting her students' tests. She did not need to look at the screen because she knew the sequence of images by listening to dialogues that she remembered from having seen the same programs multiple times. They would sit in silence because most conversational topics she wanted to pursue Donald would ignore. He would have an expression of annoyance on his face, a clear sign that he was not interested in talking. He would continue staring at the TV and chain-smoking his Kent cigarettes. When Claire finished correcting tests, she would leave the family room without Donald noticing her absence. She often wondered if he had lost all interest in her. The only interruption that he allowed for was her description of the following day's dinner. He wanted to know which cut of meat or fish she bought and how she would prepare it, warning her not to overcook it. Claire would reassure him that the meat would not be too dry, using the same recycled sentences that he wanted to hear.

"I'll make sure to take the roast out of the oven fifteen minutes earlier than the last time" or "I will leave the salmon almost raw, don't worry. If you don't want to eat the salmon, I can pan-seer tuna instead."

Whenever Claire was planning to try a new recipe, Donald would request a detailed explanation pertinent to its ingredients and spices as well as a rationale as to why some of them she could omit because he did not like them. Claire would lose her patience, and their initial calm conversation would escalate into loud verbal exchanges, she claiming to know how to cook and he challenging her assertion. Gradually she became tired of those confrontations and of cooking, which she once used to enjoy. The absurdity of their fights lay in the fact that while eating everything on his plate, Donald continued to fuss about what was missing in a particular dish that would make it better. Claire would listen to him complaining between bites but didn't react anymore because she knew that contradicting him would lead to another fight, and she was tired of that as well. He was indifferent to vegetables, potatoes, and rice, and skipped salads. Bread and meat were his favorite foods. There were only a handful of dishes they both liked.

Eager to find more information related to Peter's death, Claire rushed to her computer, hoping to find more details about it in the local newspaper. Donald's emotional detachment from the whole event didn't surprise her, but her own lack of empathy stunned her. Her once easily triggered emotions were missing. She realized that her curiosity over the particulars of Peter's disappearance in the deep of the Gulf of Mexico eroded her feelings of a loss, and admitting it made her sad because she became aware that her indifference equaled that of Donald's. The newspaper reported that the Cessna circled aimlessly above the Gulf, and a Coast Guard plane was unable to help the pilot who seemed unconscious. They could not see him well through the fogged windows of his plane. The Cessna continued to circle until it used up all the fuel, and then it plunged into the sea. The plane and the pilot's body were never found. There were no other passengers on the plane, and the police notified Peter's wife and his three adult children about his passing.

Claire reentered the family room and relayed the content of the article to Donald. He looked at her irritated because she had cut into watching one of his three programs. When she stopped talking, he made no comment and continued to gaze at the TV. Claire returned to her study feeling resentful. She felt this prevalent emotion after each attempt to revive some kind of communication between them. She thought that perhaps reciprocal annoyance was the only feeling left in their marriage.

Peter's bizarre death raised more questions. Claire felt an urgency to understand his unexpected passing, which represented an anticlimactic ending to the successful professional and private life he led. She found an old photo album with several pictures of Peter the last time they had seen him. One of them featured him at the wheel of his speedboat and cruising across one of Mississippi's canals. He had the broad smile of a content man. The photo also showed Claire's and Donald's children, eight and two years old, sitting on their father's lap, and him holding them tightly as if to protect them from falling into the water while Peter was increasing the speed of the boat. The happy picture reflected the good relationship that Claire and Donald enjoyed at that time. They hardly ever fought and lived like any young, passionate couple that was planning their future.

They visited Peter because he had offered a partnership job to Donald. They wanted to see if they would like to live in the South. Donald considered the position but after they saw the area, they both decided that he should not accept it. The salary was good, but the town where they would be living was too small, the humidity and the heat were oppressive during the long Louisiana summers, and the pesky mosquitoes flew everywhere. Regardless of the circumstances, Claire and Donald enjoyed their trip. One day when Peter was at work, they cruised on a steamboat on the Mississippi River and strolled on

Bourbon Street. In one restaurant, they ordered raw oysters thinking that they would be tastier than those they could buy back home. They couldn't eat them because they were too large and flavorless. That evening, Peter brought home several pounds of boiled crawfish bought from a local fisherman. He covered the large kitchen table with a newspaper and spread the crawfish across it. They all picked the meat out of the shell and ate it with still warm white bread. Claire remembered her sticky and smelly hands after their dinner was over.

She found another photo of Peter taken near a small lake. Claire recalled that she, Donald, and a group of their friends gathered there one Sunday. The picture showed Peter staying near the muddy looking water with his right arm reaching the top of his head and pressing down his thick, dark hair. He was short with a stocky build, and the photo revealed his hairy chest. He looked relaxed and happy. Claire thought that he was the handsomest of all the other men at that picnic. She stared at those two pictures for a long time, and sadness began to surface along with other memories of him.

Peter, his first wife, Greta, and Donald were high school friends, and they remained close throughout college in spite of their belonging to different social circles. Greta grew up in a politically affluent family, Peter enjoyed the wealth generated from a successful family business, and Donald's background was intellectual and financially modest. Peter and Greta dated each other since their teenage years and married after graduating from college. When Claire married Donald, after a few months of dating, she became a part of their group. Their frequent gatherings evolved around barbecues in summer and playing cards in winter. They all had stressful jobs, small children, and mortgages to pay. Spending time together meant leaving daily challenges behind and just enjoying the moment. The food and drinks were always plentiful, and conversational topics were trivial. They would laugh, making fun of each other and of themselves because they knew their strong and weak points. Donald was chubby his whole life and unable to stay on any diet, Greta tried to achieve a more svelte figure, and Claire was longing for designers' clothes that she could not afford. Peter was soft-spoken and a master at telling dirty jokes without sounding vulgar. The women would roll on the floor and cry from laughing even before he would reach the punch line.

Claire also remembered Peter's love of cars. During his marriage to Greta, he owned an older Jensen, in addition to two other cars. He took the Jensen apart and scattered its pieces throughout their garage. He used most of his free time learning about them and trying to reassemble the car. Greta felt left out of Peter's life more and more because he was becoming increasingly reclusive. He also liked speed. After their divorce, he moved to Louisiana, and as soon as he became wealthy, he bought his first small plane. What Claire found intriguing in Peter's character was the contrast between his mentality of a simple man who wore cheap clothes and was able to eat left over bean soup for several days and his need to buy luxury vehicles of transportation. She didn't consider him a snob, just a boy-man with a large collection of expensive toys. Peter never met Greta's expectations to become sophisticated and a member of an exclusive country club. He preferred his garage, grilled pork chops, and a cold Budweiser. After having failed to reconcile their differences, they divorced after twenty years of togetherness. They both remarried and relocated to different parts of the country. Claire and Donald's friendship with them was over. They only had one brief encounter with Greta several years later during which she introduced her new, much older husband.

At first, Claire didn't understand how such a close friendship could dissolve in a matter of a few months. She finally concluded that it must have run its course. Altered needs and hopes in people's lives intensify their desire to change. In order to feel new again, they have to leave behind all that reminds them of their past, both good and bad.

"Peter and Greta were able to do it because their shared history wasn't enough to keep them together," she mused.

Claire's connection to her past was strong and often resurfaced in the present. It would haunt her, tie her down, make her both sad and angry, and at times she could not shake it off for days. Old grievances would upset her such as her mother's failure to send birthday cards to her only two grandchildren, and her father's continuous reference to

Donald as "that one of yours," instead of calling him by his name. He never accepted Donald into the family, and his hatred for him grew over the years. Claire's parents died when they were in their nineties, and she hoped that with them being gone, she would mellow and forgive them their self-righteousness, narrow-mindedness, and egotism. She was not able to do it. Furthermore, if someone would only mention her parents, it would trigger an avalanche of bitterness, overpowering her, and her past would become more alive than her present.

Donald's relationship with his past was the opposite to Claire's remembrance of it. He lived in the present without ruminating about his past. People, events, and circumstances glided by him as if being invisible. They did not touch him in any way at that deep level when emotions become so raw that they paralyze mind and body and lead to an all-consuming numbness. Either he was not able to feel that way or he simply chose not to.

Claire returned the album on the shelf and began to rationalize the circumstances of Peter's death.

"Why did he fly to Florida and why was he alone in the plane? He was recently married to his third wife, much younger than he was. I remember George telling this to Donald after having received the wedding invitation several months earlier. It could have been a vacation," Claire guessed.

"Why did he lose a control of the plane?" she wondered.

"He was an experienced pilot with many flights under his belt."

Clare recalled one instance, though, when Peter invited Donald and her to join him and Greta for a long weekend in Florida. A friend of his who owned an eight-seat jet would fly them there. Donald was hesitant because he was never comfortable in any size of aircraft and had never been in a small one. Claire supported his decision to decline the offer, and Peter and Greta cancelled it at the last minute. Our common instincts saved us from a probable death because Peter's friend had to crash land on an empty field because of a sudden storm.

Those who flew with him were lucky to survive and suffered only minor injuries.

"I don't understand why the windows fogged up. The investigation concluded that there was no pressure in the cabin. How did that happen?" Claire pondered, not knowing anything about aeronautics.

"Why was Peter motionless? Was he unconscious or dead? Did he have a heart attack? If it was a heart attack, what caused it, stress or cardiovascular disease, perhaps both?"

Anxiety could have been a factor. Donald found out from George that Peter was under investigation for possible business-related fraud. Claire was incredulous:

"Fraud? I don't believe it. He seemed to be such an honest man, hard working."

A doubt crept into Claire's rationale. "Perhaps his appetite for self-indulgence demanded increasingly more funds to sustain it?"

"Did he crave mundane trophies from cars to opulent homes and fancy vacations just to showcase his professional success?" Claire asked herself.

"I don't think so. Having it all, he thought, would make him happy just as it did his tireless reassembling of the Jensen. The dismantled car became a metaphor for his life falling apart and his need to put it back together. Working on the Jensen enabled him to escape into another reality that promised an emotional fulfillment and harmony he longed for," Claire concluded.

Claire recognized who Peter really was – a lonely, unhappy, and possibly corrupted man. He was accumulating frivolous objects to mask his insecurity and to fill a gaping hole inside of him. By moving from one relationship to another, from one expensive hobby to a new one, he desperately tried to flee from his self-made, chaotic existence in order to reach his inner peace. Claire finally understood what happened on that plane. She imagined Peter leaning back in his pilot seat, relaxed, looking at the clear sky above him and the blue sea below, enjoying the perpetual motion of the Cessna that reminded him of a merry-go-round and the humming sound of the engine soothing him like a lullaby. His body felt weightless and free, detached from the perilous circumstances it was in. He was not afraid or panicky. He just sat there and waited for the inevitable. Claire figured out that Peter must have purposely depressurized the cabin, knowing that this would make him unconscious before his plane would take a dive into the sea.

Her vision of Peter's death was a fitting end for his life. It had all the attributes that he loved - excitement, novelty, and daringness. She imagined that in those last moments of his consciousness, he thought of his life in terms of speed and an escape. His death was tragic, unforeseeable, and remained unsolved. However, Claire was sure that his body lay undisturbed somewhere on the seabed, and she hoped that no one would ever find it.

"Peter's final resting place was of his choosing," she concluded.

Elisa

The first weekend in November 2021, my friend Elisa stayed in my house for the last time. I picked her up at home on Friday afternoon because she was too weak to drive even short distances. She had a tough time getting into my car. It took her a few minutes to steady herself by clutching the car door and lowering herself into the passenger seat. I helped her put on the seatbelt.

"It took me one hour to take a shower and pack my clothes for the weekend. I tire so quickly," she explained her labored movements.

I tried to make light of the situation and told her that she could have skipped showering because the hot water dries up our old skin in the winter.

Once we reached my house, my husband greeted her at the entrance without hugging her as he used to do prior to the Covid-19 pandemic. The number of infected people was still on the rise and Elisa had attended a large wedding one week earlier. I found out from a friend who was a guest at the same event that forty people got Covid, which meant that Elisa was directly exposed. She headed to the lower-level bedroom where she would usually stay overnight after we had watched a movie past midnight, and she had had several glasses of white wine. I watched her descending the steps at a slow measured pace while holding tightly to the railing. As I carried her weekend bag behind her, it was obvious that the task in front of her caused her great discomfort. Elisa lay down on the bed covers, taking off only her shoes and looking wiped out.

"Elisa, just rest, and I'll call you when dinner is ready."

"Don't worry, I am fine," she tried to reassure me.

When I ascended to the first floor, my husband said firmly:

"Elisa must be hospitalized as soon as possible. Her jaundice means that her liver is failing."

Being a physician, he had quickly diagnosed her dire medical condition.

"I know. When I drove her to the gastroenterologist on Tuesday, he explained to her that her enlarged liver is pressing on her stomach, which resulted in her having heartburn for months. He also confirmed the results of her recent CT scan that showed multiple small cancerous lesions and one large growth on her liver. He agreed with the oncology surgeon that the removal of them is no longer a valid option."

I will never forget Elisa's composure while she was attentively listening to the doctor telling her that her liver cancer was terminal. Her question regarding the possibility of a transplant made me realize that she still believed in her survival. Throughout her visit, the doctor's voice was calm, warm, and friendly, while his words were squashing all hope for recovery. He asked Elisa about her life, and after she had told him of having been a substitute teacher in the Forest Hills School System, he said that his children were in the same school district. His humanity was touching, but Elisa didn't notice it because she was concentrating on her questions. They were detailed and precise, affirming that her mind remained sharp as always. Another proof of her mental acuity was her insistence on filling out the health-related questionnaire herself prior to seeing the doctor. I offered to help but she declined my assistance. While she was writing, I recognized her neat penmanship executed in small letters. It reminded me of dessert recipes she would write for me after I had eaten a slice of one of her family's favorite cakes. Most of those recipes she had inherited from her German born grandmother.

After the gastroenterologist's appointment, we headed to the garage where I left my car in proximity to the hospital's main entrance. On the way there, Elisa had to rest and catch her breath several times. She wanted me to drive her to Walgreens and CVS to buy a home administered test for Covid-19 to see if she had been infected at the wedding. Neither of those places had them. I took one look at her, crumpled on the passenger seat, and leaned her head against the window with her eyes shut. She looked exhausted, and I decided to drive her back to her house. I told her to give me a call at any time in case she needed something or just felt lonely.

"I will be fine. Andy is coming on Sunday, Will and Martha on Tuesday. My Italian friend offered to have me spend the weekend in her house."

In the meantime, her friend had a burst pipe in her rental place in Detroit and had to leave immediately to take care of it. I stepped in and brought Elisa to my house.

"Elisa, dinner is ready, come up!"

I waited for her on the top of the stairs in case she needed my help. I watched her pulling herself up one stair at a time, leaning on the railing and catching her breath. The three of us sat down at the kitchen table to eat. Elisa was never a quick eater, but this time she paused even longer before each bite. She struggled swallowing a tablespoon of mashed potatoes, a few bites of pork tenderloin, and simmered carrots. She declined a glass of white wine I offered. The conversation was strained because she spent her energy on chewing. To lighten the mood, I began to talk about our grandchildren and mutual friends. I avoided asking her any questions because by answering them she would use up what was left of her already depleted strength. After dinner, we watched a TV series that was supposed to make her laugh. Elisa had a great sense of humor and used to laugh herself to tears, but this time she didn't see anything funny in the humorous content of the dialogue. Her famous laughter was gone. I accompanied her to the bedroom to retire for the night.

She spent the following day lying on the sofa in our living room impassively staring at the TV and frequently closing her eyes as if she were asleep. On Sunday afternoon she asked me to drive her back home because Andy, her older son, was on his way to Grand Rapids. On Monday, he was able to arrange for her admission to the hospital on Wednesday. I felt relieved, knowing that she would be given pain medicine to keep her comfortable. In our last exchange of WhatsApp messages, I asked her if she was getting any medication.

"Some," was the reply that I received on Thursday.

On Friday morning, Andy called me to let me know that she was going downhill very quickly, and if I wanted to see her, I could come after the doctor's afternoon visit. On my drive to the downtown hospital, I tried to concentrate on directions on my cell phone, but my thoughts were with Elisa. While crossing the garage, I tried to prepare myself for seeing her in the final stage of her life. I wanted to control my emotions and calmly talk to her sons. When I opened the door of her hospital room, the scene in front of me became etched in my memory forever. Elisa was lying in bed in an elevated position; her jaundice was even more pronounced; her gray hair spilled on the pillow; her eyes were shut, and her mouth gaped. Next to her was Andy sitting on a chair and his brother, Will, stood next to the window. Andy told me what the doctor explained to them would happen to their mother over the next weeks or days. He recommended hospice care at home. Martha, Elisa's sister, saw that she only had days to live and insisted that she remain in the hospital.

I sat on an empty chair on the right side of the bed. I said hello to Elisa, and she opened her eyes slightly, which meant that she knew that I was in the room. I touched her hand; it felt cold, and I continued to stroke it, trying to warm it up, as if that could bring her back from her semiconsciousness.

"Elisa, they told me not to bring either *šljivovica* (the Croatian plum brandy) or *cachaça* (the popular Brazilian spirit), but I think that would make you feel better than what the doctors are giving you."

She closed her mouth, and I noticed a small movement of her lips as if she were trying to produce a smile. I kept on blabbing about nonconsequential things just to fill the air with life and lessen the aura of looming death around me. I asked Will about his studies at the medical school in West Virginia, and Andy told me about making plans to move to Texas. They wanted to know how my family was. The nurse who came into the room to measure Elisa's blood pressure interrupted our chatter. I watched her mechanical movements as she lifted Elisa's gown sleeve and explained in a piercing, commanding voice what she was about to do. I understood that she was just doing her job but, at the same time, I thought that during her schooling to become a nurse, somebody had to have taught her to be compassionate toward a dying patient instead of coming across as apathetic. Elisa needed to feel love all around her.

Andy told me that another friend of his mother was about to come, signaling that it would be better that I leave because the room would become overcrowded.

"Ciao, Elisa," were my last words to her, but I was not sure that she heard me.

I closed the door behind me and stood numb for a second overwhelmed with grief. Andy followed me, and Martha was approaching after returning from the hospital cafeteria. Seeing them both, I reached my break point and began to cry. The three of us hugged while they tried to console me by saying that they go through the same emotions throughout the day, but to no avail. I could not stop crying. I sobbed all the way driving back home. Andy's phone call came at 8:00 am on Saturday letting me know that Elisa passed away at 5:00 that morning, two weeks shy of her 70th birthday.

In the following days I exchanged several messages with him and with Martha. He informed me that the memorial would be in Elisa's favorite place to visit, Meyer's Gardens, and he asked me if I would like to deliver a eulogy considering that I was her closest friend. I agreed, but just the thought that I would be talking about her and our forty-year-long friendship made me apprehensive. I knew that my emotions would be raw, and I might end up crying in front of a room full of people unable to finish my eulogy.

While Andy and Will were organizing the memorial, I met Martha. Elisa's Italian friend invited us to her house for a morning coffee and for exchanging information about the last weeks of Elisa's life. Martha wanted us to know all the details leading to her sister's diagnosis. She recalled noticing the first signs of Elisa's weakened health while the two of them visited their father's relatives in Padua, Italy three years ago. She tired very easily, and instead of sightseeing, she opted to stay in the hotel. Martha thought that the August heat was bothering her. I witnessed the same lack of energy and quick exhaustion when Elisa visited me in Rovinj in September following the Italian leg of her trip. She was getting tired after just a short walk and had to rest several times before ascending two flights of cement stairs leading to the beachfront. I saw people older than her breezing by her. I attributed Elisa's sluggishness to the heat and to her fatigue from crossing multiple Venetian bridges carrying a heavy suitcase on her way to reach the port to catch the boat for Rovinj. I didn't voice my concerns regarding her low stamina but told her that I noticed her halted breathing.

"Elisa, you need to talk to your doctor because your breathing is not right."

"It's nothing, just my allergies, don't worry. I will ask my doctor about it."

Upon her return to the States, Elisa did see her doctor, and she told Martha and me that there was nothing physically wrong with her; her heart was fine, and the asthma was causing her labored breathing. Martha disputed her asthma claim because she was the only one in the family who had it and was treated for it. None of them knew, Elisa included, that she had been infected with the hepatitis C virus sometime in the past. She found out about it when she volunteered to give blood and was surprised to hear that her blood was unusable because of its contamination with the virus. My husband told me that the hepatitis C virus damages the liver and frequently leads to liver cancer.

Martha also talked about Elisa's life when she was young. I was not aware of many details she provided. She said that her sister used to be an outgoing, adventurous person who loved to travel and meet new people. For example, in 1975 she traveled on a cargo ship to the U.S. after having received a Fulbright doctoral scholarship for graduate study in linguistics at the University of Michigan. She also mentioned another event that illustrated Elisa's free-spirited nature. One time Martha waited for her at O'Hare Airport in Chicago, as per their original plans, but Elisa never arrived. She called her from New York the next day saying that she had met an old friend in Amsterdam while waiting for her Chicago flight. He invited her to spend the weekend with him in New York.

Being unpredictable and unreliable were Elisa's character traits unbeknown to me. I knew, though, of her planned trip across the country from Ann Arbor to California with a German friend of hers. They traveled by car, slept in a tent, and either ate at roadside diners or had sandwiches bought at delis. Martha also talked about Elisa's competitiveness. The two of them used to challenge each other by playing different games that required knowledge and creativity. I knew of Elisa's love for different word-related games, crossword puzzles, and Sudoku. She could play them in her native Portuguese, as well as in English, German, French, Italian, and Spanish.

Martha said that Elisa's personality changed after she got married and had children. She seemed, to her and to the other siblings, sad, withdrawn, and passive during her visits to Brazil. The family attributed this change in her disposition to being overweight and burdened with taking care of her household and the boys. Remembering now years when Elisa was still single, I must agree with Martha's description of her in her forties and beyond. When I first met her, she was considered a great beauty in our department – tall, slender, with shoulder-length blond hair, sparkling blue eyes, and full lips over white perfectly aligned teeth. She was serious and studious, but her vivacious side would emerge quite frequently. Her colleagues liked her, and she had many male and female friends on campus. I recall her mentioning her close friend, Peter, a couple of times. I finally met him at her memorial. During her studies, she was in a long-distance relationship with a seven-year-younger Brazilian man, but that relationship was running its course. When she described it to me, I said to her:

"Elisa, you need to leave this guy. Nothing good will come out of it. You are not on the same page. You are investing your time and energy in a man that does not appreciate you. He just tags behind you."

I am not sure if my blunt assessment of her relationship contributed to Elisa's breakup with her boyfriend a few months after that heart-to-heart conversation. I am aware of another long-term relationship with a divorced man who had shared custody of two children. This one followed the earlier breakup and ended abruptly leaving Elisa emotionally bruised. The man never told her why their relationship had no future. She was single again.

By a twist of fate, our close friend, Rich, divorced and single for about a year, told us that he had decided to begin dating. A light bulb went on in my head, and I said to my husband:

"I am going to introduce Elisa to Rich. I'll invite them to dinner. I think that they would like each other."

"Don't do it! They are both adults and serious people, not teenagers."

"Exactly! Elisa is ready for a committed relationship, and Rich must feel lonely after having been married for twelve years. They are both outdoorsy people. They love nature."

My husband just rolled his eyes, signaling that he did not approve of my matchmaking. He forgot about having been my blind date introduced to me by a friend of mine decades ago.

Elisa agreed to meet Rich after I prodded her by describing a multitude of his positive traits. Rich, on the other hand, readily accepted my dinner invitation. He was looking forward to a homemade meal and spending an evening in the company of friends. Rich was a handsome man – tall, athletic, with an honest open face and a wry sense of humor. He was not chatty but could participate in any conversation by interjecting into it his laconic commentaries. The first impression of him as rigid in posture and expression was misleading because as soon as he began to laugh, the mischievous side of his personality would surface. I heard stories about his partying days while he was an undergraduate at the University of Michigan. One time his father had to bail him out of an overnight stay at the Ann Arbor police station for causing a street disturbance while drunk. He tamed his behavior in medical school.

The dinner was an easygoing and entertaining affair. Each of us reminisced about funny events from our past, and Elisa talked about growing up as the oldest of six children. Rich mentioned his two sisters, one brother, and his father. He said that his mother died from the onset of Alzheimer's when she was in her late fifties. They both talked about their experiences of living in Ann Arbor and studying at the University of Michigan. When the conversation switched over to sports, Rich had a lot to say about the Wolverines, the university's football team. The rest of us, coming from countries where soccer is popular, knew little about football; thus, we listened attentively to his description of the team's present and past successes that placed it among the top university football teams in the country. Since his undergraduate years, he had been buying season tickets. Elisa told him that she had never seen a football game in Ann Arbor. I didn't hear the rest of that conversation because I went to the kitchen to make coffee. Since it was getting late, Elisa said that she should be heading back to Ann Arbor because she had to get up early to correct seventy-five tests the next day. Rich, who lived in a nearby neighborhood, was in no hurry to leave but, seeing my husband yawning, he decided to drive home shortly after Elisa's departure.

I saw Elisa at work on Monday, but purposely did not ask her opinion about Rich because I wanted to hear from her first. She only thanked me for a tasty dinner without mentioning him. When I invited Rich for dinner three weeks later, he was equally mum about Elisa. I figured that they were not impressed with each other, and I decided not to pursue any future matchmaking for either of them.

At the end of the school year, I left the States with our children and spent the summer in Croatia visiting my parents. We returned in late August, just before the beginning of the new school year. I met Elisa in Ann Arbor a couple of days later. At the end of our chat over coffee, her question caught me by surprise:

"How is your friend doing? I never heard from him. He had promised to take me to a football game."

I remembered then that I was in the kitchen, thus missed hearing Rich's invitation to her at our dinner in May. What surprised me even more was that he did not keep his promise. I decided to ask him about it.

"My friend Elisa, the one you had met at the dinner in our house, told me that you never contacted her to take her to a football game as you had promised. Why not?"

His face glowed in disbelief. He grinned and asked me:

"She really remembered that? I am going to call her."

At that moment, I realized that he hesitated to contact Elisa because he was insecure and feared rejection. He did take Elisa to the first football game of the season, and that was the beginning of their year-long courtship that ended in a marriage officiated and celebrated in Brazil with her family and friends in attendance. Soon after, they moved to Grand Rapids to be closer to Rich's aging father. Elisa discontinued her graduate studies. Once Andy and Will were born, she had her hands full and opted to be a stay-at-home mom instead of finishing her PhD.

We stayed connected by phone and met several times both at their house and at Rich's father's cottage at Lake Michigan. I had never seen Rich happier. He finally had a family he always wanted – a loving wife who understood him and was supportive of his different hobbies and he had his boys. Whenever we met, it was a joyful occasion. I gloated watching the harmonious interaction between Elisa and Rich as they playfully patted each other and poked fun of their often quirky behavior. I would pat myself on the shoulder for having united these two people and saved them from finding the wrong life companions. My husband still thought that I was more lucky than smart adventuring into matchmaking.

During the year, Rich and Elisa would spend more time in the lodge that they co-owned with his father than in the cottage because it took them only an hour and a half to reach it by car. The lodge had been in the family for several generations. Rich grew up exploring the surrounding woods with his brother and sisters and playing by the river that weaved nearby. Andy and Will followed in his footsteps. While they were in the lodge, Rich's father would sometimes come unannounced. Elisa objected to his intrusions because the man always insisted on rearranging things around the house about which she didn't agree. In addition, he would dictate to Rich what repairs needed to be done and the way they should be executed, excluding Elisa from the decision-making. She stood her ground and refused to be in the lodge when her father-in-law was there.

Despite their differences regarding the lodge, Elisa was fond of her father-in-law. When his second wife died, she would invite him to dinner weekly and send leftovers back with him. When it was time for him and his third wife to move to a retirement facility, she was the one who sorted the leftover furniture and miscellaneous items and prepared the house for sale. This was an extremely arduous task because Rich's father was a collector of everything from newspapers to pencils, to elastic bands, to chewing gum wrappings, just to mention just a few. He never purged the house of useless objects. Instead, he neatly stashed them in designated spaces where he could easily find them. He appreciated Elisa for the care she bestowed on him and his wife, and in his will, he left the house to her.

Throughout the years, the lodge underwent major renovations. The furnace that used to heat only the first floor was replaced by a larger capacity one to be able to keep the second-floor bedrooms warm, the wooden floors were refinished, and an addition was built to enlarge the kitchen. Elisa continued to fix the lodge throughout her health struggles, driving there weekly to supervise the work in progress. The painter was stripping the old paint from the window frames and was planning in spring of 2022 to paint the siding, damaged in the 2021 summer storm.

The place meant much more to her than just having a second home in the woods. It was the custodian of her happy memories and a cocoon that enabled her to enjoy her preferred pastimes – reading and embroidering. After Rich's passing in 2015, Elisa became the keeper of his legacy, and the lodge was an important part of it. He loved its location far from the loud and hectic urban clamor. Moreover, conservation and care for the environment were his passions long before the subject entered the sphere of public consciousness and became an item of the political and governmental agenda. He took care of the trees on the property and made sure that the river remained unpolluted. Elisa shared his dedication to nature, and together they even planted trees, shrubs, and groundcovers native to Michigan in front of their Grand Rapids house. She used to make jams from the wild raspberries growing in the backyard.

I spent two weekends in the lodge after Rich died. The first time was when Elisa asked me to join her in supporting a local restaurant that had a new owner, a young man who wanted to introduce himself to the community with a revamped menu accompanied by different craft beers produced in the western Michigan breweries. He hoped that the changes he implemented in his diner would attract locals, hunters, and tourists. Rich and Elisa used to eat breakfast there and knew the previous owner well. I agreed to accompany her. We ended up tasting too many beers which resulted in my having a massive headache the next day. We barely mentioned Rich during my visit, but I felt his presence throughout the lodge. Elisa left his fishing gear and worn-out beige hat hanging on a nail in the family room, his muddy boots stood by the pile of logs in the parking space covered only with a metal roof, and a refinished dresser in the bedroom where I slept reminded me of an antique one he had loaned us when we moved into our first house. Rich liked old inherited furniture and used to get it refurbished by local restoration specialists.

Elisa had the same attitude regarding objects she owned regardless of their size, condition, or value. For example, she hired a sandblasting company to restore and paint the rusty mailbox in front of their Grand Rapids colonial home light blue. The mailbox became a landmark for visitors because its unusual color made it visible from afar. She also had a round metal outdoor table, and the matching four chairs repainted in the same blue hue. I was surprised when I saw her replacing Rich's worn-out shirt collar with a new one that she had bought in a fabric store and mending her children's ripped clothing. It was a tedious job easily avoided because clothes on sale were plentiful at shopping malls, but she liked to do it because she said it relaxed her.

Moreover, Elisa was a collector of anything interesting she could find in consignment stores and small antique shops. Her purchases included sets of depression era glasses and dishes from the 1950s, unfinished embroidering projects that she would complete, and original ceramic plates and bowls. Some of these objects she would keep; the others she would give away to her family and friends. Every time I pass by my China cabinet, I end up admiring my set of six vintage wine glasses with sturdy green stems that Elisa had given to me a couple of years ago. A green and blue ceramic plate that I placed on a console in the entrance hall was Elisa's Christmas gift to me. I have five kitchen towels that she embroidered in delicate, colorful patterns that I never used despite her nudging me to dry glasses with them because they were very absorbent. They were her cutouts from large cotton bags used in Brazil for transporting sugar that she would buy on the open market there during visits to her family. Occasionally, I pull them out of the drawer and remember her hands executing the tiniest of stitches to create her unique design. I also recall several of her plastic containers filled with neatly sorted multicolored threads and distinctly sized needles. I consider those dish towels Elisa's art project too precious to be trivialized for drying dishes. Instead, I cherish them as mementos of her.

First time visitors to Elisa's house could easily mistake it for the home of a hoarder. There were neat piles of different items from books to magazines, to fabrics for sewing and embroidering, to assortments of CDs and vinyl records. She scattered them across all surfaces from the kitchen and laundry room counters to tables, chairs, and floors. Everything had its place, and she had no trouble finding what she needed. I realized that her compulsion to accumulate various objects and to keep those that she had inherited was part of her adamant belief that things that existed had a right to be treated with respect.

As meticulous as Elisa was in taking care of her house, in her late forties she stopped paying attention to her own appearance. She gained weight, seldom exercised despite Rich's prodding, and no longer wore attractive clothes. Her staple wardrobe consisted of an oversized pair of jeans, sweatpants and sweatshirts, masculine-looking sweaters, checkered flannel shirts, and in the winter, she would put on a dark grey jacket that looked like it belonged to Rich or was borrowed from her father-in-law. However, she continued to wear earrings, the only jewelry I ever saw on her.

"I don't care about my appearance anymore. When I am in Brazil, my family criticizes my weight and comments on my plain look. Well, I cannot color my gray hair because I had several basal cell carcinomas removed from my skull. I never used makeup, and I am not going to start now," she used to tell me after each of her overseas visits.

I understood how she felt because I knew that her looks were inconsequential to her quality of life; thus, she didn't care how others saw her. She was comfortable in her own skin, and that was what mattered to her and to me, her friend. Rich loved her regardless of her changed appearance because her substance remained intact. She was honest, loyal, and proud of him and their boys.

My second visit to the lodge was in October 2020. Elisa wanted to show me the completed addition to the kitchen. It was a one-day visit. She drove and, on the way back, we stopped at a saloon near one of the backroads that led to the lodge. The place was one of those old wooden structures where locals come to meet each other and have a beer. We ordered hamburgers from the only waiter serving just a few patrons present. She was chatty and told us about her life as a single parent and about her plans to leave the town as soon as she saved enough money. Two men dressed in construction worker garb sat at the opposite end of the counter. They looked like regular guests and were not paying attention to our conversation as if they had heard our server's life story many times before. She was one of those high school graduates living in the boonies and working for minimum wage for whom upward social mobility remains only a utopian dream.

After lunch, Elisa suggested that we visit a pumpkin farm that she knew well. I found myself surrounded by tons of pumpkins in unusual colors from yellow to all shades of green. They also had whimsical shapes, and Elisa tried to convince me to buy two with long necks.

"Elisa, I am not buying them; they look obscene. The neighborhood kids will come trick- or-treating and will see them."

"They will not associate them with anything obnoxious. Their parents might, but what do you care? These pumpkins are fun."

I bought them, of course. We laughed all the way back home. Knowing that Elisa appreciated good jokes, I would also tell her dirty ones that I had heard before. She loved them because she wasn't a prude and understood what the point was – to simply make fun of people's sex lives.

Among many things that Elisa knew how to do, she was also an imaginative cook and a good baker. She created her own recipes and would frequently share meals with her next-door neighbor, a ninety-year-old woman living alone. She would make a large pot of soup that the frail lady could eat for several days and would bring her half a cake that she used to bake weekly. Her culinary skills adhered to her life's credo that all living and inanimate things deserve to be taken care of; thus, nothing should go to be waste, especially not food. For example, in addition to making jams from raspberries growing next to her garage and from other seasonal fruit that she would buy or pick herself, she also made tomato sauce from tomatoes gathered at the farm that belonged to one of Rich's cousins. One time I accompanied her to collect them before the first frost. She handed me several grocery bags, and we began our harvest. I brought home cherry, Roma, and beefsteak tomatoes in addition to mud-covered Swiss chard and kale. Elisa explained to me the steps she followed when dealing with a large quantity of tomatoes: rinse, chop, crush in the food processor, and freeze. By adopting her instructions, I spent an entire afternoon processing twenty pounds of tomatoes and removing the soil from the vegetables. I later bragged to my family that I made the Bolognese sauce that they were eating over spaghetti with the farm picked tomatoes.

Soon after Andy and Will had left for college, Rich began to have problems with his left leg. The first sign that something was wrong occurred when he tried to outpace the incoming traffic by running across the street. He narrowly escaped being struck by a car because his leg stalled. He was not overly worried about that incident and kept up his weightlifting routine and bike rides. He attributed the weakness in his leg to two back surgeries done decades ago. The following year he began to wear a brace on it. He saw several orthopedic specialists but none of them was able to confirm a specific diagnosis because he had markers for a variety of muscle-related conditions.

In my subsequent conversations with Elisa, she did not mention Rich's leg. I assumed that whatever was wrong with it had passed. I don't remember how much time lapsed before her call in which she asked if my husband and I would like to meet Rich and her for lunch because they would be in Ann Arbor the following week. At the time, I was teaching at the university, and I thought that they were coming to campus to spend a day visiting familiar sites and getting together with us. We were looking forward to it. My husband came to my office to pick me up, and as we were walking toward the elevator, we saw Elisa rushing to meet us.

"I left Rich in the car and came to warn you that he doesn't look the same as when you saw him the last time. He has difficulty walking and uses two crutches to support himself."

Her eyes teared as she tried to compose herself.

"We came to see yet another doctor here, but we still don't have a definite diagnosis."

"Do you need any help walking him to the restaurant?" my husband asked.

"No, thank you. He will be able to do it by himself. I will park in front of the restaurant."

My eagerness to see Rich turned into an ominous anxiety. We were already sitting at the table when Rich and Elisa came. He smiled when he saw us and proceeded to walk with difficulty toward the table. Elisa helped him sit down and deposited his crutches on an extra chair nearby. I was shocked seeing a once strong, athletic, and coordinated man unable to control movements of his lower limbs. The usual question "How are you?" seemed utterly inappropriate. Instead, I asked, "How was your trip from Grand Rapids?"

"It was good. Elisa is becoming quite a good driver since I had to relinquish my driving license."

"I see. Have the police stopped you again for DUI?" I tried to make light of a tense situation.

"Yes, I fell asleep at the wheel," was a classic, self-mocking Rich answer.

Elisa turned our conversation into a serious mode:

"We saw an orthopedic doctor here at the U hospital. We still don't have a definitive diagnosis or a recommended treatment."

"Let's order lunch. I am hungry," Rich interrupted her because he didn't want us to feel uncomfortable talking about his declining health.

I watched him slowly chewing his pastrami sandwich and having a sip of wine and water after each bite. He was always a slow eater; thus, a bit more tempered pace didn't alarm me at that time. The atmosphere during lunch became livelier once we began to talk about our children, my husband's retirement, and happenings on campus. We left the restaurant two hours later. My husband helped Elisa situate Rich in their red van before she drove back to Grand Rapids. That meeting left me sad and worried because I realized that Rich was sicker than I had anticipated.

A few months passed when Elisa phoned to tell us that they got the diagnosis; it was ALS. The doctors explained to them the progression of the disease that eventually would render movement of any of his muscles impossible. He would have to always be strapped in a wheelchair. Rich told her of wanting to remain in their home to the end. They decided to build a first-floor addition behind the garage that would have a bedroom and a bathroom with a shower large enough to maneuver his wheelchair. He was actively involved in all phases of the building process from selecting tiles and flooring to choosing the orange color for the walls. This project kept his mind occupied in order not to give in to desperation. He also wanted to finish the novel he had begun to write years earlier. When he was not able to write any longer, he used voice for texting to the software.

Throughout the six years of Rich's struggle with ALS, Elisa was his primary caregiver. She took care of his daily hygiene, dressing, and eating. She prepared meals that were easy to swallow because he could choke on any large piece of food. His waking up nightly to drink water and to go to the bathroom took a toll on her because she never got enough of the restful sleep that she needed after taking care of him during the day. She never complained, but her low-pitched tone of voice and shorter than usual phone conversations revealed her exhaustion.

The addition was completed three months before Rich's passing, and he finished his novel. The last time we saw him alive was on our return home from visiting our son in Grand Rapids. We found him with his head, arms, and legs fastened in the wheelchair. My husband brought him a caramel macchiato from Starbucks because he remembered that Rich liked it. He was glad to see us and to hear about our plans to move to Grand Rapids. We noticed his halted speech because he needed extra time for breathing between sentences. Andy, who happened to be in town, was holding the cup while Rich was sipping the coffee through a straw.

Elisa called us on the day Rich died. She calmly told us he went peacefully with the boys and her holding his hands. The memorial took place in a local funeral home one month later. Elisa abided by his wishes to have Rolling Stones music playing before and after the program. The spacious room quickly filled with family members, friends, neighbors, and ex-colleagues. Rich's brother flew in from Seattle despite being extremely sick and using a wheelchair himself. Andy and Will gave eulogies, and several other attendees spoke as well. The memorial was a celebration of Rich's life, and this is what Elisa wanted. Throughout all of it she sat stoically in the first row never losing her composure, and after the program had ended, she invited everyone for lunch in an adjacent room. She gave each of us a small pot of forget-me-not flowers that Rich had planted in a shady part of their front yard.

The first year of living alone was tough for Elisa. She had to figure out all the financial matters that Rich had taken care of and declutter the house from things she had needed to take care of him. She mastered all of that rather quickly, but it took her much longer to create a life for herself. She finally reached out to her old friends and joined a local Italian American club where she met new ones. She even visited a friend in Florida and traveled to Brazil to see her family. By the time we had moved to Grand Rapids, she was ready to live her life to the fullest.

The two of us spent a lot of time together. We both loved movies, and whenever an interesting one was featured in nearby theaters, we would go to matinees to avoid the evening crowds. Sometimes we would have a glass of red wine at the concession bar before the screening or go after for an early dinner in a Chinese all-you-can-eat restaurant across the street. We also frequently met for coffee either in her or my house and would spend the afternoon chatting about a gamut of subjects from politics, to different social issues, to our personal lives. Those times she sounded like her old self – eloquent, animated, and funny. However, whenever our conversation veered to Rich, she would tear up.

"I miss him. I miss talking to him," she would justify her outpouring of emotions.

Elisa and I used to call each other multiple times during the week, especially if one of us needed any advice or wanted to voice a complaint about somebody or something. I preceded Elisa in that respect. After she analyzed my problem by dissecting it all the way to its minuscule parts, I would find a solution. Her understanding of any human condition was enviable and her empathy for those who needed her help unlimited. I tried to reciprocate in kind by driving and picking her up at the airport, and one time I accompanied her to the hospital for a routine procedure that included sedation. She knew that she could count on me for anything she needed. In general, Elisa seemed healthy except for seasonal allergies that sometimes would turn into sinus infections. Sometimes when she had trouble falling to sleep, she would have several glasses of wine while watching TV. When she realized that her once occasional drink had become a daily practice, she stopped buying wine.

The first time Elisa had mentioned her daily heartburn, I was not concerned because I used to experience that periodically after having eaten rich acidic foods. However, I urged her to see her doctor. The medicine he prescribed eliminated the heartburn, but her blood pressure became too high. She began to take a drug for hypertension. She took it for a month, but the side effects were debilitating, making her tired and dizzy. Her doctor put her on different medications, yet her blood pressure continued to fluctuate. She also had to modify portions of the food she ate because she felt full fast and had a sensation of heaviness in her stomach as if her digestion was halted. To demonstrate to me the amount of food she was able to eat in one meal, she pulled a small cereal bowl out of the kitchen cupboard. She stopped drinking coffee, her preferred beverage, throughout the day. She tried to reschedule her December appointment with a gastrointestinal specialist for an earlier date but was unable to do it.

I left for Croatia at the beginning of July. During the summer we emailed. Elisa would describe work being done in the lodge and her health problems related to her still high blood pressure and her difficulty digesting any food. The day after my return to the States at the end of September, I called her to set up our meeting because I knew that she would like to hear about my stay overseas. I was surprised when she asked me if I wouldn't mind if we postponed seeing each other because she had not been feeling well in the past three weeks.

"Of course. No problem. Just give me a call when you feel better."

At that moment, I realized that there was something terribly wrong with Elisa. Two weeks elapsed when she finally contacted me.

"I'll be in your neighborhood this afternoon. Do you have some time for me?"

"Of course, just come over. Any time is good."

When I opened the front door, my first look at Elisa confirmed my fears that she was sicker than she had led me to believe. Her face was covered in red blotches, and when she smiled, her teeth seemed larger because of her sunken cheeks. It was obvious that she had slimmed down. I hugged her and couldn't stop myself from telling her:

"Elisa, you lost a lot of weight!"

"Not that much, only about 5 pounds."

By looking at her she was at least twenty pounds lighter. I also noticed her protruding stomach.

"I don't know why my stomach is sticking out as if I am six months pregnant."

"Elisa, you must ask your doctor about it. Ask her why you continue to lose weight. It is not normal."

"I did. She ordered different tests, and they all came out okay. My heart is fine, my blood pressure is more stable, and my cholesterol is low. I don't know what else to do."

After that visit, I would call Elisa daily because each time after having asked her how she was feeling, she would say:

"Every day a bit worse."

Finally, her doctor sent her to get a CT scan. As soon as she had received the results, she forwarded it to me, and I showed it to my husband. Elisa finally got her diagnosis – she had liver cancer. From her diagnosis to her passing it was barely over three weeks. I was left with a lingering question if she could have survived given an earlier detection. My husband explained that maybe she could have lived a bit longer, but eventually she would have succumbed to cancer. He added that the speed of her decline saved her from the difficult, often devastating side effects of chemotherapy; thus, it shortened her suffering.

Since Elisa has died, there is not a day that I don't think about her. I miss talking to her, discussing world events, and exchanging complaints about everyday living. Going to the movies without her has lost all its appeal for me. I keep the memory of her alive because she was such a big part of my life. I still haven't erased her WhatsApp messages and emails, and I am saving all handwritten recipes she gave me. I also neatly sorted photos of her in one of my albums. I will always love Elisa because she was a quality person, complex and yet simple, endowed with smarts, wittiness, at times oddness, modesty, sincerity, and generosity. But her most endearing and memorable asset was her humanity. She left a lasting impression on all those who crossed her path not only because of the wealth of her knowledge that she so generously shared but also because she valued everyone and bestowed on each person her full attention, making him or her feel accepted and appreciated.

Elisa was a people person, and, perhaps, living as a loner, Rich held back her nature, and this can be attributed to the sadness her family saw in her, as if he unintentionally had burned one of her inner bulbs. I, on the other hand, prefer to remember the two of them as forest wanderers, sandcastle builders at the Lake Michigan shore, and aficionados of the Mai Tai with the fresh floating orchid in hand sitting on the beach of one of the Hawaiian Islands they so loved.

Grand Rapids, December 2021

Marina Vlady

Whenever I think about the meaning of friendship, my thoughts flee to the French actress Marina Vlady, a daughter of Russian immigrants. You might ask what a connection between an actress and my take on friendship could be. Of course, I have never met Marina, and I no longer remember any of her films from the 1960s, but the image of her etched in my memory reminds me of my best friend and of her looks at the time I met her. She had Marina's mid-shoulder-length blond hair, slightly slanted brown eyes, high cheekbones, and full lips. She was tall, meaty and voluptuous, and strikingly beautiful. In a way, she appeared like a better version of Marina perhaps because of the beauty of her untouched Slavic features, unlike those of the actress that were minimized by her yielding to the demands of French sophistication.

In spring, fifty-four years ago, I saw my friend in a small theater for the first time. It was the opening night of Ionesco's play, *The Bald Prima Donna*. The crowd in the theater lobby included colleague actors, theater directors, drama students, and an audience interested in less conventional plays. I came alone. My actor boyfriend met me at the entrance and handed me a free ticket. He pretended not to know me for the rest of the evening and joined his fellow actors in a lively chat during the intermission. I got used to that behavior of his and didn't mind cruising around the lobby by myself. I was too young and a novice at dating to understand how insulting his conduct was. I noticed my "Marina" just a few feet from where I stood surrounded by her friends, laughing aloud, and having a wonderful time. I stared at her, unable to look elsewhere. She didn't notice my gaze, which would have embarrassed me. As soon as the play ended, I returned home, while my boyfriend stayed behind and spent the night drinking with his friends.

At the time, both "Marina" and I were first-year students studying Comparative Literature at the University of Zagreb. The following day, I was supposed to attend the first class in a lecture room that could accommodate one hundred students. I arrived on time but there were only a few empty seats left. While trying to find one, I saw "Marina" doing the same thing. Simultaneously, we both spotted the only two available seats next to each other in the last row. We rushed to claim them before somebody else snatched them since we saw several other students still entering the room.

The well-known professor began his introductory lecture by explaining the difficult path that the discipline of comparative literature had to pass through on the road to acceptance as an academic field. He drew the comparison between epistolary novels disputed as a literary genre until the 18th century and comparative literature. "Marina" and I took notes and occasionally nodded to express our understanding of the professor's lecture. We did not introduce ourselves and spent the hour in silence. I wanted to know "Marina," and decided to approach her when the class was over. I took the risk of presenting myself as an ignoramus by asking her:

"Did you understand anything that he was saying?"

"Not a word," she answered.

My question and her reply were the beginning of our long-lasting friendship.

"Marina" suggested that we go on foot to the downtown area instead of taking a tram. This was the first of our daily walks from the university building to her family's apartment situated in the heart of the city. In subsequent months I frequently spent afternoons in her spacious three-bedroom apartment on the second floor. Its large windows faced east and the street, while the balcony overlooked a forested park on its west side. The place was full of antiques, valuable paintings, Persian rugs, and hundreds of books. It was the most luxurious apartment I had ever seen. Furthermore, it also had a small room adjacent to the kitchen for the housekeeper, Rafaela, an old maid dressed in black, with a protruding upper jaw that hindered her speech. She had lived with "Marina's" family since her teenage years. Rafaela was very protective of my friend and used to send away those young people that she didn't like. She warmed up to me and would bring us a lemonade when we were studying together.

Beside Rafaela and "Marina" there was only her mother, a university lecturer, living in the apartment. "Marina's" architect father died when she was in high school, and she did not have any siblings. Looking at her living surroundings, one could easily conclude that she grew up in privileged circumstances. I, on the other hand, was a product of middle-class parents, both working high school graduates, righteous, and often narrow-minded. We lived downtown in a turn of the century two-bedroom apartment whose windows were only four feet above the pavement and covered with iron security bars. Despite our different social status and upbringing, we found common ground in the fact that we were both single children. This was important in the first years of our friendship because we would share our experiences in finding friends when we were children, learning how to communicate with the outside world, and discovering ways to avoid feeling lonely. Neither of us had to share or fight for toys or the affection of our parents. We understood each other perfectly.

"Marina" got married to her high school sweetheart in the sophomore year of college and had a son in the same year. She and her husband finished their undergraduate and graduate studies and pursued their careers in academia. I got married one month after receiving my graduation diploma, and two years later, I moved with my husband and one-year-old son to the USA. In such circumstances most friendships would have dissolved, but "Marina" and I knew that ours would overcome the distance and evolve into an even deeper understanding and affection for each other.

When I am in town, we meet as often as possible. We talk openly about things that matter to us without censoring our thoughts as we tend to do with other people. Our trust in each other is ironclad. Our fears and sorrows are in the open, our hopes spelled out, our rage not hidden; we negotiate and try to minimize hurts that come to us from others, and we advise each other and bury our secrets. We are each other's shoulder to cry on, and we laugh hysterically at our own jokes.

We even created a unique vocal modification in our talks to which only our husbands are privy. We address each other by the same name "Milica." The time we spend together always seems too short; thus, we avoid inviting other friends to join us. If by accident someone stops by while we are sitting in a café, we feel like the intruder is robbing us of our precious hour together. We are both too polite to openly ask him or her to leave. Instead, we stall the conversation to the point that the unexpected visitor realizes that we want to be alone.

"Marina" is very skinny now, has a bit of a curved back, has been wearing a short honey colored haircut for years, and wears glasses. She still has the same contentious laugh, flirts with anyone around her, hasn't lost her irresistible charm, dresses in the latest fashion, and walks in flats as she did in our college days. As we both have gotten older, our talks focus more on health issues, vitamins we need to take, and exercise we should do, but the emphasis is also on facial creams, lotions, and other remedies that would make us look younger. After a bottle of a good red wine, we really don't care about it any longer and conclude that our principal enemies in life are mirrors and bifocals. "Marina" is more than my best friend; she is my soulmate.

Sara's Birthday

I was sitting in Barnes & Noble sipping my macchiato when Sara approached me and handed me the white envelope. She was smiling broadly, while I could not hide my surprise.

"Please sit down, Sara. What is it this?" I asked her without opening the envelope.

"It is an invitation to celebrate my eightieth birthday next Sunday," she explained.

While Sara got comfortable in her seat across from me, I read the invitation. It was professionally designed with black lettering stating the place and time for brunch.

"Thank you, Sara. I'll be happy to come."

"I am glad that you can make it because I want you to meet all my friends."

I looked at Sara's white cotton, long-sleeved blouse with a sparkly broach attached to one of the buttonholes below her neck and her short blond hair probably self-coiffed with different size plastic rollers. She projected an image of a dignified, elderly person who took care of herself because she didn't want to be seen as an old fogey who turned away from life. Her bright blue eyes and sunny disposition reminded me of why we became friends several years ago despite her being three decades older than me. Sara's cheerful outlook expressed through her curiosity about world affairs and her desire to learn new things made her into an interesting and delightful collocutor.

We met at the same Barnes & Nobel where I used to browse through newly published books and magazines a few times a week after having finished teaching my last class in the early afternoon. Sara would come daily to read the *Paris Match*, *Der Spiegel*, and *The New York Times*. I noticed her because she seemed out of place among students in hoodies and boho clad middle-aged readers. Her age was not the only attribute that distinguished her from the present crowd. It was her wardrobe I recall the most. She would always appear dressed appropriately for each season. She wore classic style clothes with only a few of the vintage details revealing that she had purchased them years ago. They reminded me of my mother's '70s outfits that she still wears because she claims that their quality is superior to the Chinese-made garments sold in shopping malls. Despite her surroundings, Sara looked perfectly comfortable and would march straight to the magazine and newspaper stand to fetch her usual reading selection. Her steps were a bit awkward as if she had problems with her hips, but the reason for her ungainly stride could have been also her weight. She was overweight for her short stature.

On the day we first met, Barnes & Nobel was packed and all the seats at the small tables were taken. I was sitting alone at my table in the far corner away from the others. Sara spotted me and asked:

"Excuse me, may I join you?"

"Sure!" was my laconic answer because I was deep into organizing tomorrow's lecture.

"Thank you! I will not disturb you."

After she spoke, I lifted my eyes from the computer for the first time and instantly recognized her.

"I remember you. You are frequently here."

Sara's face lit up with a smile. Perhaps being noticed meant something to her as it would to those who go through life unnoticed, not by choice but by circumstances.

"Sorry, I don't remember you. I am Sara. What is your name?"

I noticed her thick accent and concluded that it was of Slavic origin.

"Renata. Nice meeting you!" I extended my right hand and shook hers, which had an unusually firm grip for a person her age.

"I noticed your accent. Where I you from?"

"I am Russian, from Mosca. I emigrated to America together with my son in 1980."

"Does you son live with you?"

"No. He is married and lives in Atlanta. He teaches mathematics in one of the community colleges there," she answered matter-of-factly.

From her unemotional reference to her son, I figured that they were not very close.

"Sara, where do you live?"

"I have a studio apartment in a retirement home built for Russian immigrants of Jewish decent. It is nice to be able to speak Russian and have friends who understand you because we share the same past and negative experiences while we were living in the Soviet Union."

This was the only time during our years-long friendship that Sara mentioned the Soviet Union. I had a feeling that she was unable to shed the fear of somebody from her homeland eavesdropping on all her interactions with other people which could still jeopardize her and her son's American citizenship. The fear of the KGB's spying methods was deeply ingrained in her consciousness.

When she finished browsing through a stack of newspapers, she said:

"I have to leave now because I am meeting my friend to see a movie together. See you on Sunday."

"Bye, Sara. See you on Sunday!"

The rest of the week passed quickly, as did the many others that made me feel like it was always Friday. Sara's invitation stated that her birthday party was taking place in the pricey and elegant Gandy Dancer. The restaurant, a restored 1886 Michigan Central Depot, was the city's historical landmark. Its large windows facing railroad tracks enabled diners to watch the passing trains. The place was known for its brunches and seafood entries. Sara reserved a smaller room separated from the main dining room because she wanted to have a more intimate celebration. Moreover, she knew that her friends would have prepared birthday toasts that could disturb other patrons.

I arrived first and found her already sitting at one of the four round tables that could accommodate ten people each. Soon afterward, I saw her friends wriggling between dining room tables and booths to join us. I noticed that other diners stopped eating to stare at them. The reason for it was their over-the-top attire that clashed with the modest Sunday brunch wardrobe of other guests. It made them look out of place and bizarre. As they were getting settled in their seats, I was amazed both by their deliberate moves and their clothing. I guessed their age being between sixty and seventy. Among them were more women than men. Women wore black and navy cocktail dresses decorated with rhinestones around the collar and muslin or lace-covered long sleeves. Golden jewelry gleamed from their ear lobes, necks, and fingers. Their blond and reddish dyed hair was perfectly coiffed, and they wore more makeup than one would expect from women their age. The men were clad in suits, white shirts, and ties. Sarah in her dark green jersey dress and I in my button-down blue dress with the small white flowers blended well with the rest of the restaurant crowd. I think that getting dressed to the nines was her friends' way not only to honor the occasion, but also to recall times when they used to go to concerts, operas, and different festive events in their native Soviet Union. Sara's birthday was their nostalgia moment.

When everyone was seated, the waiter invited us to a self-serve display of brunch food. I sat next to Sara, and we both waited for others to fill their plates first. Several long tables covered with crisp white linen tablecloths brimmed with meats from carved ham and roast beef to chicken. There was also salmon lox, steamed mussels, shrimp, herring, salads, vegetables, fruit, cheese blintzes, and an assortment of breads. For those who preferred breakfast food there were hash browns, bacon and sausages, scrambled eggs, and eggs benedict, as well as made-to-order omelets and Belgian waffles. A variety of desserts along with coffee and tea were at the very end of the display.

When the people at our table returned, I marveled at the quantity of meats, different vegetables, salads, and breads on their plates. Sara's had only a few items on hers. I think that she was overly excited and lost her appetite. The waiter came by again asking what everyone would like to drink, and most of her friends ordered a glass of champagne. I watched them devour their food with gusto. They would only pause when one of them rose his or her flute to toast Sara. I was expecting that after such a substantial meal a lively conversation among all present would follow, but I was wrong. Her friends went for a refill. This time their plates were covered with hash browns, bacon and sausages, differently prepared eggs, and Belgian waffles. Sara didn't join them for seconds but was delighted to see them liking the food.

The third trip to the brunch table involved desserts. The first person who returned to our table was a slender woman carrying her plate packed with brownies, fudge, and slices of different cakes. I thought that she would place it in the middle of the table to share it with the rest of us. Instead, she put the plate down in front of her and proceeded to eat all the sweets herself. I watched her both amused and amazed wondering about the digestive capacity of her stomach. Suddenly it dawned on me what the reason was for her and Sara's other friends' voraciousness. They all grew up in the 50s and 60s, remembered as the years of food shortages in Europe. This scarcity of food especially affected countries with autocratic governments such as the Soviet Union. They lived on staples, such as bread, milk, sausages, vegetables, and locally grown fruit while well-paid government employees shopped in groceries that carried caviar, imported cheeses, and French wines. Their generation experienced hunger when the staples were not resupplied; thus, they felt that their very survival was in jeopardy.

I think that those who are deprived of food for a period of time in their lives never forget that sensation and the fear of being hungry again never goes away. For Sara and her friends not even the American groceries, known for their abundance of comestibles at affordable prices, could eradicate that fear. An opportunity to eat an unlimited amount of food free of charge triggers in them a primal instinct for consuming as much of it as possible, just not to feel hungry again. As the whole brunch scene unraveled in front of me, I realized that once being famished impacts both a person's conscious and unconscious mind and leads to his and her state of never having enough. Ultra-rich and misers subscribe to the same mantra of "nothing is ever enough," which makes them fearful of losing their wealth which they consider essential for their well-being.

Sara's birthday celebration was a huge success among her friends, and she seemed to enjoy every minute of it. It was a lavish affair for which I am sure she had to save money the entire year. She didn't want any presents, but I felt that her son's attendance would make her happy, but he never came. I was glad to have partaken in that joyful event.

"Thank you for inviting me, Sara! I had fun! See you at Barnes & Noble next week."

As I drove back home, sadness overwhelmed me because I had met a large group of people who late in their lives voluntarily uprooted themselves from their native land and settled into the new American reality of plenty that still could neither bring them into the fold nor free them from their past suffering and deprivation.

The Letter to Mila

Dearest Mila,

May 10, 1979, 3:30 am, was a special day in both our lives. You drew your first breath and left me breathless in awe as I looked at your pink, plump little body being placed on my nude belly in the delivery room. You even smelled pink. Your pudgy, round face turned red as you let out your first cry. You stretched your arms in the air as if you wanted to touch my face. Your delicate fingers and fingernails were also pink, but your feet had a darker shade of it. I thought that the pink traveling from your upper body to your lower extremities simply changed its hue. You were my Little Miss Pink. I almost cried, moved by your loveliness, but was too exhausted to express the emotions that overwhelmed me. My eyes followed the delivery nurse lifting you from my stomach and beginning to bathe you. I was afraid that she would wash off all the pink from my baby, but she didn't. When the bathing routine was over, you stopped crying and fell asleep in her arms. Your gender surprised everyone, especially your dad, but not me because I knew to have carried the first girl after four generations of boys born into your father's family.

The following thirty years have passed in a flash, all memorable because of you, and all gratifying to me as your mama. I hope not to have made too many mistakes raising you, but if I have, it was unintentional. I tried to guide and protect you as you moved through different stages of your life. I promise to correct all my wrongs in the next thirty years. You have a forgiving heart, one of many admirable attributes that comes to mind if I am to describe you to someone.

The other day I came across a story that I began to write on the eve of your eighth birthday but left it unfinished. I decided to go back to it after a twenty-two-year hiatus because I think it would be a fitting gift for your thirtieth birthday. The stars aligned this year, and your birthday coincides with Mother's Day. We can both celebrate.

Little Miss Pink

Livonia, 1987

It is May 6, four days before Mila's eighth birthday. The excitement had been piling up since her last one because already the day after her seventh birthday, she was planning how she wanted to celebrate her next birthday. From the time she learned how to count, she would add one more girl's name to her guest list so that their number would coincide with her age. I hope that she does not continue with this tradition as a teenager.

Mila wrote and handed out all her invitations in early April. They featured a brown, dancing bear on the front page and details about the place and time of the party on the inside. Unfortunately, one of her little friends is unable to come because of a trip with her parents. Having only seven instead of eight girls present didn't spoil her future fun. Today, after Mila returned from school, we went to Toys "R" Us to buy birthday plates, napkins, paper cups, and party favors. She selected her tableware with Little Pony on it and wrote the girls' names on each birthday goody bag saving one for her absent friend. She filled them with colorful sunglasses, shimmering bracelets, stickers, and two kinds of candies. We didn't buy balloons because neither my husband nor I have the strength to inflate them. Mila has chosen the VCR movie her guests will see and decided on the menu: pepperoni pizza, Coca-Cola, and for the grand finale a chocolate cake. She has planned her birthday party to the last detail.

As I expected, my Little Miss Pink will wear her pink dress because pink is her favorite color. Her preferred stuffed animal, a miniscule rabbit that she found one year in her Easter basket, is also pink, as is her Barbie, a sexy blond in a long pink gown. Mila's favorite jacket is pink, and all her barrettes are pink as well. She paints her life pink.

All grown-up

Los Angeles, 2009

January 09 was especially frigid in Michigan. Each day snowbanks grew larger by newly fallen snow and gusting winds. Most of the time the sky was metallic gray and overcast, obscuring the rare patches of blue that tried to break through the thick clouds. Every morning I dragged my feet out of the warm bed to face another seemingly endless, snow-laden day. I stopped watching the weather channel because the images of other states buried under mounds of snow would put me in an even worse mood.

With February approaching and with it my spring break from teaching, I decided to visit Mila in Los Angles where she lived. I found a cheap flight and was looking forward to my trip. I am one of those people who love to fly. For me it is not just traveling from point A to point B and back. It is rather a means of escaping from my daily routine, to experience something new, to discover what is hidden, and to abandon myself to a feeling of freedom. There are people afraid of their autonomy because they don't know what to do with it; thus, they prefer that somebody else presents them with different options. I am not one of them because I create my own choices – some of them are interesting and energizing; the others begin as such but eventually become boring, and I replace them with more stimulating ones. My mini vacation in LA always lifts my spirit not only because of the aforementioned reasons but because time spent with Mila is invaluable.

As soon as I kissed my husband goodbye at the Detroit airport, I was in the zone. I boarded the plane, sat near the window, my chosen place on all flights, and looked at the airport baggage handlers loading suitcases, carry-ons, and duffle bags. I had an early afternoon flight. Dark clouds saturated with rain droplets hovered around the sky, but they couldn't dampen my spirits because I knew that blooming magnolias and forsythia were waiting for me across the country. As the plane soared in the air, I closed my eyes just to feel myself, not the noise and movements around the cabin. The calm washed over me. I took the crossword puzzle book out of my purse, a simple one with answers in the back, and began to solve the first page. After the third puzzle, I became bored. Then I read the airline magazine which quickly bored me as well. Being bored is a luxurious state of mind for me because my daily multi-tasking often robs me of this self-indulgent waste of time.

The flight lasted five hours. As the plane approached Los Angeles, I watched the city lights spread across it. The early evening sky was indigo. When we landed and started to roll toward the designated gate, I called Mila. She was driving on her way to pick me up. Her voice on the phone sounded cheerful and I was eager to see her. When I stepped on the LAX sidewalk, the balmy evening breeze made me take off my heavy winter jacket. I didn't wait long for Mila's arrival. We briefly exchanged hugs because the pickup area bans any parking. When I entered her KIA, the mess on the back seats and the floor did not surprise me. There were different size boxes, empty bottles to be returned for recycling, her sweatshirt, and sneakers. Being neat was never her forte. Growing up, Mila's bedroom was full of different objects scattered across the floor, her bookshelves had more trinkets than books, and the bathroom she shared with her orderly, six years older brother had wet towels piled up next to the tub after she had taken a bath. Mila stuck to her childhood motto that straightening and cleaning her surroundings was a tedious and time-consuming task devoid of any creativity. When she bought a spacious condo in an old Los Angeles neighborhood, she hired a cleaning lady the second week after she had moved in.

While Mila drove, I was admiring her makeup-free fresh face and her shoulder length light brown hair. She wore a beige, pencil-cut short skirt, and a brown merino wool sweater. Her outfit was sophisticated, fitting her attorney profession. Her overall appearance had evolved in the past years, but as soon as she began to talk animatedly about different topics, her core resurfaced. She was still fun loving, spontaneous, warm, all-embracing, the daughter that I always knew. We chatted all the way back to her place jumping from one subject to the next. Our words flew uncensored as we expressed our opinions. I realized that our mother-daughter relationship had matured to an adult closeness despite our occasional disagreements.

We spent the first evening playing Wii games, Mila as an experienced professional, and I, being a novice, tried my best. For dinner she cooked corn chowder and baked tasty little buns, the name of which I have forgotten. I watched her from the living room as she zigzagged through the kitchen getting the ingredients she needed. Her moves were measured and relaxed. It was obvious that she was comfortable putting together a meal. I knew that she loved to entertain and that her parties often included several dishes that she would prepare herself but seeing her actually in action was a new experience for me. I credit myself for having taught her by example that good company, a home cooked meal, and a bottle of nice wine are all part of living a full life. It is gratifying to recognize those bits of self in one's adult child. Mila also perfected the art of mixing different cocktails, which I never learned because my husband's and my friends were wine and beer drinkers.

My LA week passed quickly. Every day was different. When Mila was not at work, we drove to furniture stores looking for a bedroom set. We found a modern one in black mahogany wood. In an outlet we bought two white leather bar stools and in Bed Bath & Beyond we found silk draperies to cover her bedroom window. She took me to the best sushi restaurant in town, had lunch in an Argentinean restaurant, and ate hamburgers in Father's Office, a Los Angeles landmark gathering place. She made a reservation for a cozy Italian osteria to celebrate my March birthday early. I invited two of my Michigan friends to join us. They moved to LA a few years ahead of Mila. She also showed me her fancy downtown office. The entertainment highlight of my visit was the play *Rent*, which we saw together with my son-in-law. I enjoyed the actors' superb performances.

Each day in LA was one more precious pearl that I added to my memory string because I realized that Mila was so much more than just being my child. She was a tender and loving wife, a helpful friend when her girlfriend's car broke down during the morning rush hour and she needed a ride home in the evening, and a respected professional. She took on all her roles with grace and a dose of humor. However, two images of her that replicated her childhood habits endeared me. Every morning, she rose after turning off the alarm clock, put on her short, fluffy white robe, and sat down with a bowl of cereal or a waffle in front of her. Her eyes were half open, and her hair was messy, but she looked sweet and innocent as if her original pinkness had returned. The second image repeated itself each evening when she would lie next to her husband on their white leather sectional ready to watch her favorite TV program. It reminded me of her early childhood ritual of leaning against her father's plump stomach while he was stretched out on the family room checkered sofa. In that position she would fall to sleep. Regardless of years past, evenings still enabled her to lose herself in the moment, shut out the outside world, and ignore life's daily chores. Dirty dishes piled up on the kitchen countertop and the bedroom floor covered with her only once worn clothes didn't bother her. For her those were only unimportant details of daily living. She was right. I wish I had learned that when I was younger. Sometimes I feel like my daughter's pupil.

My departure date came quickly. As always, I was sad to leave Mila. Being near her makes me immensely happy. I do miss her terribly and sometimes resent the fact that she moved from Michigan to the other side of the continent. As we exchanged our last hugs, I was at a loss for words and barely able to utter "Thank you." I rushed to enter Delta terminal, and didn't even turn around to wave goodbye because I didn't want her to see me crying.

I am on the plane again. Window seat. It's midnight, a red eye flight to Detroit. I am thinking about my daughter. My heart swells with joy realizing how much of Little Miss Pink is still part of her. She continues to color her world pink because it is a color of innocence, sweetness, warmth, and playfulness. These attributes described her when she was eight and have simply morphed into her present self. She added to them her fearlessness in pursuing new ventures and taking the road less traveled. However, she doesn't act on them without prior research of the odds stacked in her favor or against. She is passionate about a variety of endeavors from creative writing to art projects, to competitively playing pool. In her view the world is a large playground of infinite possibilities. She is a complex woman that is one and the same rational and emotional. A kind word and a gentle gesture can easily move her. Our family and her friends benefit from her thoughtfulness. She despises narrow-minded and malicious people and decisively removes herself from their orbit.

Does Little Miss Pink have any shortcomings one might ask? Being her mother, I am the wrong person to answer. If she does have any, they are only bits of darker colors that quickly disappear in the immense sea of pink that surrounds her. My daughter is the greatest gift that ever fell in my lap.

Love, Mama

THREE

Homes

In the late '70s the States' ranch style house with a detached garage, two bedrooms, a family room, one and a half bath, and a basement symbolized upward social mobility as opposed to a rented apartment. It was called a starter home. The down payment for the first mortgage emptied John and Karen's saving account, thus there was no money left to install automatic yard sprinklers, and dad's gift of his old lawn mower was greatly appreciated. Friends and relatives donated their unwanted furniture describing them as antiques. Pretty soon the once empty house amassed objects with a history and the sentimental tokens of someone else's life, and with it was transformed into an eclectic style home. The non-strippable wallpaper with hideous red flowers and green parrots were reminders of the 60s interior along with pink- and taupe-colored tiles in the bathrooms and yellow kitchen appliances. Despite an obvious disparity between the unique features of the house, the place radiated harmony and joy because the young couple adopted its shortcomings as if they were of their own making.

The starter home began to weave its own history. There were many firsts – the 4th of July barbecue with old friends, the next-door neighbors who welcomed them into the neighborhood with tomatoes from their garden and brownies, the New Year's celebration, and the birth of the first child, a boy that they named Patrick. An older couple three houses down the road even offered to babysit. The first raking of falling leaves from the large maple and oak trees on the front yard took the whole weekend, and the purchase of a snow blower was an unplanned but necessary expense.

The second child followed a couple of years later. As time passed, John replaced the wallpaper in all the rooms with semigloss white paint. The midnight blue ceiling in the second bedroom took a primer and three coats of white paint to cover it. The couple fondly remembered their first fight because it involved buying a new couch for the family room because the donated one was falling apart, according to Karen. Her husband was vigorously opposed to it as he was to other purchases of new furnishings. One example of his frugality regarding anything that he deemed nonessential was their daughter's nursery furniture. Their friends loaned them a crib after their daughter had outgrown it. Since they were expecting their second child, they wanted it back.

"John, we have to furnish Emma's nursery. The Bakers are coming to pick up the crib next Thursday," Karen warned him on Saturday.

"We should just buy a twin bed and put pillows around her. The chair next to the bed would keep them in place," he calmly said looking her straight in the eye, as if his suggestion was an acceptable solution.

"Are you insane?! She is four months old! She needs a crib, a dresser, a changing table, and a bookshelf for her baby books and stuffed animals." Karen's voice was stern as she relentlessly pressured John to agree with her.

"Okay. Let's go shopping tomorrow," he grudgingly consented.

What unnerved Karen the most was John's resistance to purchasing household items that didn't directly serve him. He was eager to buy things that only he considered essential such as a stereo system, a computer, and the latest television model that he would turn on as soon as he entered the house after work. He often left it on even during his hours-long naps after dinner.

After their quarrel, Karen waited the whole month before she opened up a discussion about the new sofa. This time she added to her wish list a rectangular coffee table, two velvet covered side chairs that she recently saw on sale in Hudson's, and a small oriental rug. She mentally prepared herself to keep calm while explaining to John her reasons for wanting these furnishings. He reacted with a resolute "No!" and she lost her composure. John saw Karen's wishes as redundant while she considered his selfish. After that fight, they didn't talk to each other for several days. Eventually, each got what they wanted because they were taking turns in giving up on their demands.

After having lived sixteen years in their starter home, John and Karen moved into their second house. They had established careers and earned good wages. Moreover, the house became too small for their growing children who wanted to invite their friends for sleepover parties. That second house was a significant upgrade in comparison to the first one. Karen found one of the last empty lots in a newly built suburban neighborhood and hired a well-known architect to design their new home. The sloped backyard stretched all the way to the nature preserve wetlands and a pond. From their large cedar wood deck, they could hear birds chirping and frogs croaking in the spring. Their front and back yard were professionally landscaped and lit, and the automatic sprinkler system was on a timer so as not to waste water when it rained. The lawn care company mowed the grass on Thursdays and fertilized it four times yearly. Every other Monday the cleaners would come to dust, vacuum, and scrub the three bathrooms and polish the black granite kitchen counters.

Life was good. The Weber grill was fantastic, and John became a true pro with a barbeque fork in his hand. Friends would come over to celebrate the 4th of July and Labor Day in September. History repeated itself in just more prosperous circumstances. Vacations in exotic destinations were affordable, and the household purchases were no longer topics of quarrels. Amid all that bounty, they suddenly had to face challenges that they put aside while pursuing their material comforts. Both sets of parents were in their eighties and needed help. Furthermore, Patrick was in graduate school and could not afford to buy a car to drive to his classes, and Emma was a junior in college. John and Karen knew that their family depended on them. They assumed a united front and dismissed whatever was left of their wants. They organized in-home help for their parents, bought a stripped-down small Toyota for Patrick, and paid Emma's tuition and living costs on campus.

After getting steadily higher electrical and water bills for heating and cooling their five thousand square foot, two-story house with a finished basement, they concluded that as empty nesters they did not need all that space. They loved their home because it was truly theirs as they watched it being built, from the pouring of the foundation's cement to layering the brown shingles on its roof. They decided to spend a few more Michigan muggy Augusts in their home. Both felt that it was not yet their time for downsizing.

Once in a while, John and Karen talked about their future after they retired. They agreed that their last residence should be a scaled down house, not a condominium because the word alone they associated with institutional living. The idea of moving to Florida, a traditional destination for many Michigan retirees, didn't appeal to them because as John said:

"I don't want to be surrounded by old people who drive 50 mph on the freeway."

Karen was afraid of Florida's six-month-long hurricane season. They were certain to build their next house from scratch because it should have all the specifications satisfactory to their future needs. They envisioned in it their children's engagement parties, wedding brunches, and grandchildren's baby showers. There would again be new beginnings. Life is full of firsts, and this is how it should be. Years melt away like an ice cream barely licked, and the end creeps up unnoticed.

Balconies

I used to visit my parents once a year after I moved to the United States in 1974. Having a full-time job did not allow for more frequent visits. They lived in former Yugoslavia, today Croatia, and my summers spent with them enabled me to see socio-cultural changes that took place when the country became independent and transitioned from communism into capitalism. Usually, my flight would land at Zagreb Airport in the afternoon. I would take a taxi to their apartment, a short thirty-minute ride during which I would chat with the driver about the latest news in the city and across the country. Those cabbies were like the pulse of the entire nation. Their views on politics, the economy, and the wellbeing of citizens were more insightful than what the TV news presented, and newspapers wrote about. I heard their uncensored comments on society, absent during the communist rule, and understood them as a first step toward democracy that should foster and protect freedom of expression.

While the driver would unload my luggage on the sidewalk, I always had a feeling that behind each curtain-covered window of that four-story building neighbors were watching my arrival. They were curious to see who would exit the cab, luxury transportation for most of them. I would feel like an intruder into their close-knit social group, but only for the first several minutes. One of the neighbors would always show up on her balcony, greet me, and ask how my trip was. Her welcome would make me feel at home.

My parents lived in their apartment for half a century, and after they had died, I became the new owner. I stay in it for several months in summer, but I don't feel like an outsider anymore. I belong to that nosiness-ridden community of neighbors. The building is an ordinary box-like structure typical of the communist era architecture, plain and unadorned. It has three separate entrances and three apartments on each level, and every apartment has a balcony. Some neighbors have enclosed theirs with glass panels to gain more footage in their fifty-six square meters of living space. The others keep them open to store things that don't fit indoors. Those open balconies sometimes have hanging baskets for flowers, like my mother used to have, and they are preferred locations for cigarette smokers who the family bans from puffing away in the living room. However, their principal function remains for hanging the laundry to dry in the sun.

The apartments are frequently inhabited by a family of four, thus crowded, but nobody finds anything unusual about it. The concept of privacy doesn't infringe on their daily routine because members find his or her own tiny space that suffices for his or her need for seclusion. I always think about those family arrangements as efficiently organized chaos that work well more often than not. Being close to someone takes on a completely new meaning in these dwellings because parents and children are close in both a physical and emotional sense. Their lives are entwined into a spider-like web that is hard to break. The perfect harmony among members is seldom achieved, but nobody expects it anyway. Togetherness is an economic necessity because many employed adult children cannot afford to rent or buy their own apartment on their salary. Thus, they are forced to live with their parents even after they get married. Grandchildren are welcome as well. As the parents age, their middle-aged offspring take care of them until they die, and then the apartment becomes theirs. Depending on any changed circumstances in each family, the balcony assumes different purposes: for example, an angry family member can decompress on it, grandchildren often turn it into a play area, and in the summer, the balcony becomes a tanning salon and an entertaining spot for celebrating birthdays, graduations, and promotions.

As my parents got older, they faced several age-related health issues, from my father's multiple surgeries to my mother's dementia. I often felt guilty about living far away and not being able to take care of them personally. They functioned well on their own until their late eighties when my mother decided not to leave the apartment anymore. She was probably afraid of getting lost and not remembering how to return home. In late spring, during summer, and in early fall, she used to spend hours on their balcony sitting on a large wooden box covered with an old, checkered green blanket. My father kept his tools in it, half of them rusted; the others were missing parts, thus not usable. She would sit staring in front of her, smoking her cigarette, and getting up only to look at her flower baskets. She had a blank expression on her face because most of the time she didn't know what was going on around her. My father was the one who bought their groceries every day. My mother in her lucid moments would remember that he went shopping, and she would wait on the balcony for his return. She would see him carrying in one hand a plastic bag containing two liters of mineral water, a carton of milk, a loaf of bread, and one kilogram of bananas, his favorite fruit, and in the other hand he would lean on his cane to help him walk after two hip replacements. He would enter the apartment drenched in sweat from climbing stairs with this heavy load. Neighbors witnessed his struggle, and several of them offered to bring them groceries but my mother refused their help. She rejected their kindness because they belonged to the building that she loathed.

I remember that when we first moved into our new apartment from a downtown turn-of-the-last-century three-story house, she hated the fact that she had to take a tram to go downtown. It didn't matter to her that this new residence was on the second floor, had a balcony and large windows overlooking a park with a merry-go-round and monkey bars, a central heating system, a tiled bathroom with running warm water, and a showerhead above the deep ceramic tub. She longed for our old, street level downtown apartment – where anyone tempted to spit straight into our living room would have been able to do it – for the green tile-covered fireplace that had to be fed with chopped wood and coal in order to warm up two bedrooms, and for the bathroom that had a copper water tank that we had to heat manually by burning old newspapers in it. Every Friday, a bathing day, I was in charge of the latter. The second and third-floor apartments had balconies facing the busy street, thus they couldn't be used for hanging laundry. My mother and other neighbors would hang their clothes on ropes stretched between the two walls in a small courtyard. They had to agree on the days when each family could use it. In the winter, everyone dried their laundry layering it on their fireplace. Despite all these shortcomings of the old apartment, my mother never missed an opportunity to reprimand my father about how wrong he was in accepting the new one from his employer - the government.

Since my parents retired in their early fifties, they had plenty of free time to monitor happenings in their new location. Their balcony became my father's observatory post. He would rush to it each time he would hear someone parking a car close to his used five-year old Volkswagen Beetle. He was afraid that one of the neighbors might scratch it by parking too close and carelessly opening the driver's side door. Once he noticed a deep gouge on the Volkswagen's hood, and my mother accused our next-door neighbor's son-in-law of keying it, just to spite them. I think that my father probably bought it already scratched but was afraid to admit it to my mother. He let her badmouth the young man for several years. My mother's ire was also directed toward my father because she had given him money to buy a new car after their old Fiat 750 was no longer safe to drive. Instead, he drove home a used old clunker with worn-out upholstery, windows that opened only halfway, and a radio that didn't work.

My father developed an additional habit besides guarding his car from the balcony. He would zoom to the apartment's entrance door peephole to watch people ascending and descending stairs. I never understood why this spying on neighbors entertained him. I guess this was his way of silently connecting with their lives because in person he only related to them with a simple "Hi." Despite my father's social awkwardness, he developed a friendship with a widower near the middle entrance to the building. The two of them shared a passion for the game of chess, and they would play it for hours several times a week. My father would set the chessboard on the dining room table in such a way that the two of them were able to face each other. Neither of them was competitive, thus they would praise each other's effective strategic moves. When the weather was warm, the door to the balcony was open, and they could see my mother sitting on her bench and smoking. As much as my father loved those afternoons with his chess pal, she hated them because she felt excluded. She pestered him with warnings that sitting for hours was bad for his hips. After his friend died, my father continued to play chess. As a longstanding member of the Croatian Chess Federation, he was able to compete at chess tournaments for seniors and often won them.

My mother was more sociable. As soon as they moved into the new apartment, she became friends with the next-door neighbor. The woman's apartment was smaller than my parents' apartment. It measured about forty-five square meters, and her balcony faced the east side of the building. This way she could see who was walking from the tram stop toward the building and at what time. I never understood why she and my mother found this monitoring of other people's movements to be an interesting enough topic to discuss. The neighbor was my mother's age, a retired seamstress who used to sew costumes for plays in one of Zagreb's theaters. She was slender, had wavy, gray, shoulder-length hair, delicate-looking hands, and wore thick glasses. Even after her retirement, she continued to sew, but only for a few people, mostly altering their clothes. She was married, had one daughter, a son-in-law who was an architect, and a granddaughter. The young family lived in the same size apartment just one flight above hers.

My mother would drink coffee with that neighbor on the balcony every day. They would alter balconies depending on which one of them was alone in the apartment. When my father was grocery shopping, coffee hour took place on our balcony, and when her husband was paying bills at the post office, they sat on hers. The two women would chat about their youth and their present lives. The neighbor told my mother that the city gave her family those two apartments after the Sava River had flooded their home a few years earlier. I remember that flood because many families who lost their homes slept on cods in my high school while waiting to be placed in permanent residences. This friendship lasted until my mother accused the neighbor of having stolen our bed sheets while we were on vacation. She gave the apartment keys to the woman to look after it and water flowers on the balcony while we were gone. After that allegation, our neighbor stopped talking to her.

My mother had an especially hostile relationship with a neighbor directly across from our apartment. The middle-aged, heavy-set woman, with bleached blond shoulder-length hair and a cigarette hanging from one side of her mouth, lived in it with a much younger man. It seemed that neither of them worked because their car never moved from their parking place, and they seldom left the apartment. Despite it, neighbors witnessed continued improvements taking place in the apartment. My mother also noticed a horde of people, mostly women, coming in and out of it. She concluded that the woman must have been running a bordello as the principal source of her income. This neighbor once knocked on my parents' door to borrow a pack of cigarettes. She probably saw my mother smoking on the balcony. The woman never brought back a new pack, and that unnerved my mother. She would get angry whenever she remembered that incident. She also accused this neighbor of having stolen a plant she left in the corner of a flight of stairs that led to our apartment. I don't know who stole my new doormat while I was gone last year, but I doubt that it was this woman. To make sure, I checked hers; it looked worn out, and it was not mine.

Since I have been owning the apartment, I have not noticed any unusual traffic to and from the apartment across from mine. The man is gone, but the remodeling work continues. The neighbor below the woman's apartment told me about it because the constant banging on her ceiling and other noises from above bothered her. They were especially loud when the woman was enclosing her balcony with glass panels and installing aluminum shades over them. That first-floor neighbor casually mentioned that the woman is running an escort business out of her apartment. I burst out laughing because at the time I thought that my mother was getting loony accusing her of such an illegitimate enterprise. Nevertheless, I have to admit that in this case she hit the nail on the head.

My parents rarely spoke to the neighbor in the apartment below theirs. The woman moved into the building much later than other people did. Her son was just a boy when my father saw the two of them in front of their apartment for the first time. Years later the woman showed up at my parents' door to tell them that their bathroom was flooding hers. She wanted them to repair the damage done to her bathroom ceiling. My mother called me a long distance at five o'clock in the morning to inform me that there was a problem with the plumbing in their bathroom. I called a friend of mine to help me out as he had done it many times in the past. He sent a plumber to my parents' apartment, and he discovered that my mother caused the leak by having thrown paper towels into the toilet bowl instead of toilet paper. I attributed this incident to her galloping dementia.

After the bathroom situation was resolved, I offered to have my neighbor's bathroom painted. When I discussed this with her, it was the first time that I met her son. At that time, he was a high school student. He looked like a typical teenager, tall, skinny, with the latest style of haircut – spiked on the top. He said "Hi," and instead of leaving his mother to talk to me, he proceeded telling me about having met my father when he was a boy. He also wanted to know how my mother was and showed an unusual interest in both my parents and me. This was not a conversation one would expect from a teenager, even a polite one. I thought that there was something odd about him. I asked the first-floor neighbor if she knew anything about this young man. She told me that he was caught exposing himself in front of the elementary school nearby. The police came, witnesses were credible, and his mother was ordered to keep a close watch over him and not let him wander around unaccompanied. Now when I am on the balcony, I only see his mother hanging laundry and never notice him. She covered the balcony floor with nice ceramic tiles and replaced the old hanging rods with expensive steel aluminum.

Across from this neighbor lives a woman who has my apartment keys. Over the years she became a good friend. She is the one who checks that everything is in order while I am gone: she makes sure that the heating units are functioning properly, collects our registered and regular mail, and pays bills that we cannot pay through online banking. My friend is in her early seventies, has blond hair cut in a neat bob, dresses in jeans and oversized cotton tops, and walks a bit hunched over. She has lost a lot of weight in the last couple of years because of her reoccurring health problems. I see this as an ominous sign that she is sicker than she lets me believe. She deals with her condition stoically, never complains, follows her doctor's orders, doesn't allow it to take over her life, and believes that she will overcome it. She takes care of her household, and as a retired teacher she still tutors the high school seniors in preparation for their college entrance exams.

Furthermore, my neighbor friend is also the caretaker of our building. She collects the association's annual dues, makes sure that the house is in good condition inside and out, and successfully solves problems that neighbors sometimes have with their, now privately owned, residences. People were able to buy their apartments from the city below market value in spite of getting them free from the government decades earlier. By selling the apartments, the city governance collected money from its citizens to replenish its empty treasury. However, nobody knows what happened to that money. My parents also bought their apartment after cashing in German Marks that my father had earned one summer when he worked as a tennis trainer in Germany. Those of us that enclosed our balconies also had to pay the city for building permits and additional taxes for the gained square footage of usable space. Many of these new owners moved out and rented their apartments. Only a handful of old neighbors remain. I have only met the renters next door, a young couple that have been living in the building for several years. I see them once or twice during my stay in Zagreb when they exit their apartment in the morning, but I never see them sitting on their balcony or hanging their laundry.

When I am in town, my neighbor friend and I always go to one of the nearby outdoor cafes to have cappuccinos and talk about events that happened since we last saw each other. The most intriguing news she tells me comes from the neighborhood because she knows each household very well. She is an animated narrator, and I am never bored listening to her. She also has a great sense of humor that captures my attention even more. My friend lights several cigarettes while waiting for cappuccinos to arrive because her husband doesn't allow her to smoke in the apartment out of concern for her health, he tells her. She thinks that he, an ex-chain smoker, is super sensitive to the smell of cigarettes. However, when he is out and about, she sits in her striped canvas covered lounge chair on the balcony and smokes. I think she did not want to enclose their balcony precisely because of that habit of hers which she does not intend to get rid of.

For other neighbors, glass paneled balconies were fast and relatively economical solutions to add more living space to their small urban dwellings. They also do not require any upkeep, such as painting of the rails and doorframes, and do not need frequent sweeping. The open balconies, on the other hand, are extensions of lives happening behind them. Each day at least one family member steps on the balcony to check the weather or hang the laundry. Some shake dust rags at midday while the neighbor below has an open window or throws a fruit pit on a patch of grass next to the narrow sidewalk. If the balcony's door happens to be open, discussions that are taking place inside an apartment could spill into the street for all passersby to hear. For the heated arguments most of the neighbors stay on their balconies pretending to be doing something and not listening. The topics of those quarrels are then discussed among the listening crowd over morning and afternoon coffees. When the sudden downpour threatens to soak semi-dry clothes on the drying line, there is a rush on each balcony to pick them up. In winter, open balconies hibernate until early spring.

I view those balconies as living organisms in perpetual motion because their functions change from sunrise to sunset, from month to month, and from one season to the next, and yet they never lose their primal identity as places where one hangs the laundry. They witness joys, sorrows, anger, and compromises because they share the lives of each apartment dweller. They breathe life into all its predictable and unexpected moments. My house in the States does not have a balcony. Instead, it has a deck that the blue jays and robins use for sitting on its railing. My home is a fortress that lives only within its walls. My neighbors' houses are replicas of mine. We know each other's names from the subdivision directory, and we meet twice a year to discuss how to spend the yearly association dues. The privacy of each owner is carefully safeguarded. Gates to our subdivision close after dark and can only be open with assigned numerical codes. I don't know anything about my next-door neighbor except that in the summer, the family erects a handball net, and the husband prefers to cut their grass instead of hiring a professional company that does ours. Our homes are luxury enclaves, far from being organisms that make me feel alive and belonging to the fellowship of human beings. Our alienation gives us a sense of security but strips us of life's pulsating beat that the open balconies offer in abundance.

Old Neighborhoods

For some people a visit to their old neighborhood can evoke unpleasant, sometimes traumatic memories of events that had taken place years ago. They remember run-down houses, unkept lawns littered with broken toys and garden furniture, rusted trucks and cars in driveways, and neighbors drinking a six pack of Budweiser on their porches. They recall police, firetrucks, and ambulances announcing their arrival with their ear-piercing sounds, and their mothers' 911 calls in the middle of the night. There are others who used to live in well-groomed and safe suburbs where neighbors waved to each other while walking their beloved pure breed canines holding them tight with decorated leather leashes in one hand and plastic little bags for their feces in the other. The serene outdoor image sometimes belied what was taking place inside their luxury homes, ranging from parents' vicious alcohol and opioid induced fights that occasionally would end up in a physical altercation to mental and physical abuse of their children, all of which would lead to the destruction of the family structure. These people's recollections are equally painful when they pass by their old neighborhood.

I, on the other hand, love to visit the area where I lived as a student. My studio apartment with a balcony overlooking a park and a playground with a sandbox, a slide, and a jungle gym was on the second floor of a red four-story brick building that beside mine had another eleven units, three on each floor. A tall oak blocked my view of the same style building across the park and shadowed my balcony during the sweltering summer afternoons. During my four-year-long stay in it, I met most of my neighbors, but only three of them would invite me to their apartments for a cup of coffee. They were Mrs. Z from the first floor, Mrs. V next door to me, and Ms. D above my studio.

I was Mrs. V's frequent visitor because of our proximity to each other and, I guess, she liked my company. She was a seamstress in her early sixties, slim, and slightly hunched over from years of bending over her sewing machine. Her short, thinning gray hair was neatly coiffed, and her pale face was full of deep creases and fine lines around her lips. The frame of her glasses stopped in the middle of her nose. There was something dignified in her demeanor. During one of our coffee klatches, she told me that she used to sew costumes for one of the largest theater companies in the city, but once she retired, she only sewed for her only daughter and granddaughter. Her daughter and son-in-law lived in a one-bedroom apartment above hers. They had a daughter that Mrs. V babysat since she was born because both parents worked and hiring a nanny would have been costly. To make the young couple's lives even easier she would also prepare dinners for them.

Mrs. V married her high school sweetheart soon after their graduation. I seldom saw her husband because she would invite me for a coffee when he was doing grocery shopping; thus, I would only encounter him on the staircase. I remember him as being a short, chubby man with a protruding lower jaw. Years later, I read his obituary which disclosed Alzheimer's disease as the cause of his death. They also had a son, married, and without children. His apartment was above his sister's. Mrs. V told me about their son's heart problems for which he had been hospitalized a couple of times; thus, I was not surprised to see him exiting an ambulance while I was opening my mail sitting on a bench in the park. What puzzled me was the fact that he was walking toward me instead of entering our building. He asked me if he could join me on the bench.

"Sure. Sit down, please." I thought that his heart condition had worsened, and I asked him:

"I saw you being brought by the ambulance. How are you feeling?"

His answer caught me by surprise. "Thank you for asking. My heart is relatively okay. I had to go to the ER because my wife threw two crystal ashtrays at me, and one of them hit me on the head causing a gash that needed stitching."

I didn't ask him what the reason for his wife's violent outburst was, but the worried expression on his face when he was describing his injury contradicted the expected reaction of being angry or offended by such a physical assault. I understood his anxiety and his delayed return home after Mrs. V told me later that day that he had cheated on his wife with his brother-in-law's younger sister. His wife learned about it and went into a rage. Regardless of the seriousness of the event, and my condemnation of any form of domestic violence, I imagined the sequencing of the whole scene, and at the end found it very funny. Years later and married, whenever I would retell this neighborhood story to my husband, we would laugh ourselves silly.

One time I asked Mrs. V for the reason that her entire family lived in the same building.

"I don't know if you remember the big flood ten years ago. The river S overflowed its high banks, and our entire neighborhood was wiped out. We stood on the roof of our house for several hours until the rescue crew saved us. The insurance company reimbursed us for the lost property, and with that money we were able to buy all three apartments."

"I remember that flood. The city government placed those who lost everything in my high school. They converted classrooms into a temporary shelter and filled them up with cots."

Years later, my husband and I visited my old neighborhood curious to see if anything had changed in terms of new construction, cafes, and grocery stores that I used to go to. He parked in front of the building where I spent my college years. We spotted Mrs. Z sitting on her balcony. She recognized me and I immediately introduced my husband who waved to her. She greeted us with her unforgettable warm smile and said:

"Welcome! Oh, my goodness! I haven't seen you for the longest time! Come upstairs for a cup of coffee!"

"I don't want to bother you. We were just driving around our old neighborhoods remembering people and events that took place when we were younger."

"No bother, at all! Come upstairs!"

Mrs. Z asked us to sit at the table in her dining room adjacent to the kitchen, while she heated water for an instant coffee. When she joined us, my first question was:

"What is new in the building? Who stayed and who moved out?"

"After Mrs. V passed, her daughter sold her mother's and her apartment and bought two detached condominiums. The larger one she gave to her daughter and her family, a husband and a daughter, and the smaller one she kept for herself. Mrs. V's son died, and his wife moved out, but I don't know where she lives now."

"Who is living in my studio now?"

"The same man to whom you had sold it, but I seldom see him. He keeps to himself."

I mentioned to Mrs. Z that I noticed several new grocery stores and cafes and praised the upkeep of our building.

"The new manager of the Association is very diligent and quickly resolves all problems that owners have in their units."

I looked at Mrs. Z across the table and noticed that she was sipping water instead of coffee. I knew that she had a transplanted kidney and was on a strict salt-free diet, but I wasn't aware that she had to give up all caffeine-based beverages.

"Mrs. Z, you no longer drink coffee?"

"The doctors told me that I have to stop because my transplant is over twenty years old, and that soon I would need to be on dialysis."

Mrs. Z was in her sixties, retired from her teaching job in a nearby high school where she taught math and calculus. To subsidize her modest pension, she gave private lessons several times a week. Despite her persistent health problems, she never complained, took care of her household, and was a legal guardian for her younger schizophrenic and diabetic brother who lived in the same neighborhood. She managed his finances, washed his clothes, bought him food for the whole week, and organized a daily delivery of a special dinner for diabetics. She would also administer his prescribed medicines three times a day. She told us of finally getting permission from social services that allowed her to commit him to a mental institution without his consent when the schizophrenic drugs failed to control his outbursts. Mrs. Z didn't like to talk about him, and I never asked, but when she would open up, she was more angry at him than compassionate. I guess years of taking care of her brother after their mother, his primary caregiver, had died took a toll on her nerves.

I was glad that Mrs. Z's husband was not home during our visit because I remembered him being very annoying. I always tried to avoid a conversation when I saw him on the staircase ascending or descending or meet him in a grocery store while we both waited in line to pay. He used to suggest that we walk back home together, and those were times that I was unable to wiggle myself out of the situation. He would tell me his life story that I already knew by heart.

"I never graduated from college but was lucky enough to find a well-paid job in a large construction company. You know, I used to drink a lot with my buddies at work. Before I married Z, I enjoyed life to the fullest."

This is a condensed version of his monologue that he would expand on with a litany of dull, repetitive details told in a monotonous voice and with a slight stutter. He never changed, neither the sequence of his sentences nor a single word in them. His soliloquies also got on his wife's nerves. To block them she used to put on earphones. I can picture her walking around their apartment with sound protection gear on her ears and him following her without stopping talking, a comical scene by all accounts.

Mrs. Z's husband was ten years older than she was, and must have been tall when he was young, but when I met him, his back was a bit curved, and he walked haltingly. He was still driving his old Toyota but only to the open market on Saturdays and his wife to the hospital when she felt sick. He and Mrs. Z never had any children because of her early onset of health problems.

"I forgot to ask you about Ms. D? I noticed her balcony door shut."

"After her retirement she spends several months at her sister's. I haven't seen her for a while."

I remembered well Ms. D. She was slim, had average height, and her flame-colored short hair framed her puffy face. Large brown eyes were the most prominent feature on her visage. The puffiness and the gray skin tone of her face were typical for an alcoholic, which she was. Whenever she would invite me for a cup of coffee, she would offer me a shot of cognac from a half empty bottle sitting in front of her. It was her preferred drink, which I could smell on her breath as soon as she greeted me. She used to talk about her sister and her nieces and nephews that she adored. She never mentioned being married nor any other man in her life. However, she did not lack male companionship. Sometimes, late in the night, I would hear whispering voices, hers and a man's, passing by my door on the way up to her studio. She got along with other neighbors, and in kind they never gossiped about her lifestyle.

Mrs. Z briefed me about other neighbors that I didn't know well. I asked her to give me the address of Mrs. V's daughter because I was planning to visit her and thank her for coming to my parents' funerals. Mrs. Z wrote it on a piece of paper along with her cell number. Our visit lasted longer than anticipated, and it was time to leave. I noticed my husband's eagerness to put an end to it when he got up first. I understood that Mrs. Z's and my conversation didn't interest him because he was not invested in my old neighborhood, nor did he have any emotional attachment to his. His neighborhood was a place where he ate, slept, and studied. Mine was intertwined with personal relationships and a memorable environment; it was a nurturing surrounding during my formative years. Before leaving, I hugged Mrs. Z and promised to keep in touch.

"Please, don't be a stranger. Next time you have to tell me all about yourself. "

I knew that she was sincerely interested in my life because we shared part of our past, and were more than former neighbors, we were friends.

The next day, I called Mrs. V's daughter. She was surprised to hear my voice and readily agreed that I should visit her the following week. When she opened her door, I stood in front of a short, gray-haired woman in her fifties. Her face was pale and heavily lined as her mother's had been. Their resemblance was uncanny. This first visit was the beginning of our yearly get together.

Her condominium has a large terrace full of potted flowers that I look at while sitting at a round table in her den. We talk about our old neighbors, our deceased parents, our families, and age-related health issues. She usually offers me a glass of white wine and different snacks. She told me that she has to stop drinking coffee because of high blood pressure. We look at each other and read emotions that cross our faces. We listen to diverse pitches in our voices, talk in sentences that flow uninterrupted, and create true human contact. Our frequent bursts of laughter always scare her miniature white poodle that leaves the den and hides in the other room. Those visits are always meaningful to me because they give me a sense of continuity, a feeling that my past stretches into the present and on into the future.

Old neighborhoods always remain part of our identity, both the one that we would like to forget and the other that makes us nostalgic and determined to safeguard it.

Plumbing by Jim

In the second year of living in our new house designed by a well-known architect and built by a reputable construction company, we encountered the first plumbing problem. The kitchen faucet was dripping with an annoying sound of single drops falling into a ceramic sink, and the garbage disposal stopped working. Our architect gave us a reference booklet with the names and addresses of different tradesmen that we might need in the future, but there were no plumbers listed. While picking up the *Detroit Free Press* from the mailbox across the street, I found a handwritten flyer with the name of a plumbing company. Eager to solve my plumbing issue, I called the cell number written on the flier.

"Hi, my name is Romana. I have a problem with a dripping faucet in the kitchen and the garbage disposal is not working. Could you come to fix it? I live in Northville."

"Hi," a deep voice answered.

"How did you get my number?"

"I got it from your flier left in my mailbox."

"Oh, that was my girlfriend who wrote it and distributed it in the new subdivisions. She insisted that I advertise my services. Give me your exact address. I can come after five today."

"Great! See you then."

I couldn't believe that any plumber would come on the same day. It was not a convenient hour because I usually prepared dinner at that time, but I adjusted my routine in order not to lose him. At five o'clock sharp, the bell rang. I opened the door to a tall, skinny man, in his forties with piercing blue eyes and sparce blond hair. He wore jeans that hung low on his hips and a white T-shirt. He stretched out his hand for a handshake. His grip was firm and reassuring.

"Hi, I am Jim. I own the plumbing company you called. I am installing plumbing in a new subdivision nearby, so I can help you only after my regular hours."

I led him into our kitchen and showed him the two problems I had. He decided to fix the faucet first. Without explaining what he was going to do, he unscrewed the faucet and pulled a plastic container full of different size rubber rings out of his toolbox. He took out one of them. I couldn't see where he placed it because I stood four feet away from him to give him space to work undisturbed. Then he fastened the faucet back to its position and turned the water on and off. The leak was gone. After he took out the garbage disposal, he seemed eager to clarify what was wrong with it.

"The builder sold you a lemon. It's junk. I will buy the best one for you at my supplier and will install it tomorrow after five."

"Super! Tell me the cost of it and what I owe you for your work."

He quoted his fee for both repairs and quoted the price for a new garbage disposal. Both charges were very reasonable. I would not have negotiated them even if they were higher because I appreciated his professionalism and the speed with which he fixed my faucet and diagnosed the garbage disposal problem.

"You can pay me for everything tomorrow."

The following afternoon, Jim showed up carrying a box with my new garbage disposal. Again, he worked in silence. It took him one hour to install the garburator. He arose from his kneeling position and looked across the countertops to find a piece of vegetable or fruit to test its grinding. He spotted a lemon that I kept together with fruit on a large metal platter.

"Cut a slice of that lemon and throw it into the sink."

I obeyed his order. He turned on the water and the garbage disposal switch. I heard the grating sound of the lemon slice being ground into a pulp. My new garbage disposal served me well throughout the next twenty-two years.

While I was writing a check to pay Jim, he began to tell me about several of his customers who had faced the same garburator problem as I did. He described in great detail the complications involved in replacing it because it was difficult to find models that would fit the existing plumbing. I handed him the check, but instead of leaving he stayed for another fifteen minutes talking about his clients' demands regarding the selection of a new garbage disposal.

"Their line of questioning really unnerved me. They didn't know anything about garbage disposals and what was available on the market."

He also mentioned that some of them would argue about his fee after he had already completed the work or would postpone the payment by telling him that they would mail his check. He didn't like that at all and would drop them as customers. I watched Jim talk. His monologue became increasingly animated as he pointed out things that irritated him in dealing with difficult clients. I was not sure if that was his warning to me not to behave as they did or if it was his attempt to personalize our, to that point, strictly business relationship. His soliloquy also included boasting of being a plumber who could solve any problem related to waterworks. I began walking toward the entrance hoping that he would follow me. Indeed, he did, but his story ended only when I opened the door wide.

In later years, Jim was a frequent visitor to our home. Diverse types of leakage and cloggage surfaced affecting other faucets, our two refrigerators, and the shower stall in the finished basement. The worst one was a complete flooding of the lower level caused by a faulty valve of the hundred-sixty-five-gallon water heaters. At that time, we were traveling, and our friends were house sitting; thus, they had to call our insurance company and organize the emergency flood removal services. We left them Jim's contact number. He came the same day and shut off the other water heater. When we returned from our trip, he suggested replacing both water heaters with a tankless one because by doing that we would never again have to deal with a flooded basement. In addition, this new one would be energy-efficient because it would heat only the amount of water we needed. A couple of days later, Jim installed our tankless water heater.

Whenever I needed his help, I would phone him and repeat the slightly altered but virtually the same line I had given him the first time I had contacted him.

"Hi Jim. This is Romana. My kitchen faucet and the garbage disposal (refrigerator, shower stall, toilet, and so on) are leaking. Can you come?"

"Hi, Renata. I'll be in your house at five."

In each of my calls, Jim would rename me. I became Rinona, Erica, and Debby. I never corrected him because I didn't mind his modifications of my identity. I began to imagine the person I could be behind one of those names. For example, as Rinona, I saw myself as a Southern Belle who likes country music and line dancing; Renata sounded very European; Erica could be a CEO in a large company; and Debby stood for a homemaker with four children who watches daytime soaps and drinks beer in the evening.

After several years of working as a master plumber for different construction companies, Jim resigned from his last job.

"They wanted me to use substandard plumbing features and materials in luxury homes. This is not how I operate."

Knowing him, I understood that his work ethic clashed with the builders' lack of it. They looked only after their profit and forfeited the quality of homes they were building. Being self-employed enabled him to service his customers throughout the day. He was never in a rush because he considered telling stories about his plumbing related experiences an integral part of his job. Jim was a born storyteller. The topics of his monologues were leakages and clogging, not exactly interesting subjects, but with his acting-school-worthy gestures, the voice modulations, and the intense look into his listeners' eyes, he made them memorable. During his narration, I never interrupted him by asking questions because his exhaustive description of events and clients didn't call for any additional input. Despite voicing his complaints about customers who stiffed him or were difficult to deal with, he never mentioned their names. Being discrete fitted his attitude regarding their privacy.

One time he mentioned his hobby of drag racing during the weekend. Somehow this did not surprise me. He struck me as a guy who would enjoy speed and the adrenaline coming from racing other drivers after having spent the week stationed by somebody's plumbing problem. I imagined him sitting on his porch and drinking a six pack of Budweiser with his buddies following their competition. Jim had the face of a functional alcoholic, something I recognized from knowing several of them. It was a bit puffy, with red blotches and tiny red capillaries protruding under the skin. He was also skinny because some alcoholics substitute food calories with those they get from alcohol; thus, they become undernourished. One Monday he showed up with a cast up to his knee telling me that he slipped on the ice-covered steps while going to his truck. I kind of doubted his story. I think that he got intoxicated from drinking beer with his girlfriend while watching TV on the weekend. The drag car racing season was over and there was nothing else to do in winter months. He told me that once they removed the cast around his broken ankle, he would undergo three weeks of physical therapy during which he would not be working.

Of all the plumbing hassles experienced in our last house the most bizarre one was linked to our master bedroom toilet. For several weeks there was a terrible smell coming out of it. I thoroughly washed the bowl inside and out, but to no avail.

"Hi Jim. This is Romana. My toilet in the upper floor bathroom reeks of a terrible odor. When can you come by?"

"Hi, Romina. I'll be there after lunch."

This was the closest that he ever came to correctly pronouncing my name. When I opened the door, I saw him and another man standing in front of me.

"This is Jerry, my assistant."

"Nice meeting you, Jerry. I am Romana. Come on in!"

Jerry was a heavy-set middle-aged man, a foot shorter than Jim, with greasy brown thinning hair and a stubble-covered face. When he smiled, I noticed that he was missing most of his upper teeth, which made him hard to understand when he talked. We entered the bathroom, and Jim first flushed the toilet and examined it from all sides. The space behind it was narrow, difficult to reach with a mop. In an almost accusatory tone of voice, he pointed it out to me.

"A bit of dust there."

Looking at his pristine white T-shirt and socks, I concluded that he must be very meticulous in keeping not only himself well-groomed but also his house in a spick and span condition.

First, Jim asked Jerry to remove the grout around the toilet. When his assistant knelt and bent on the tiled floor, his pants slipped and exposed half of his derriere. I pretended not to notice it, and Jim didn't react, obviously accustomed to seeing Jerry's bum. Once the grout was gone, the three of us saw a gold rim on which the toilet stood. Jim helped Jerry lift the toilet and place it on a blanket to protect the tiles. The rim consisted of pennies that the builder's plumber put there to raise the toilet above the tiles instead of putting a layer of grout or asking the tile man to adjust the tiles to the required height. The result of it was that the toilet never sat properly on the wax ring and the flange. With time, both parts rotted causing the foul smell.

Jim was disgusted with the plumber's botched job, and Jerry rushed to the truck to bring the tools and materials they needed to fix the problem. I felt amused by finding out what caused the odor in the bathroom. It took them two hours to complete the work. At the end of it, Jerry's flannel shirt was soaked from his profuse sweating, while Jim looked regal in his spotless white T-shirt and dry armpits. He sported the look of a winner who successfully executed the challenge in front of him. He did not proceed to tell me a story about a toilet problem identical to mine because it did not exist. It was unique for him as it was for me, but I am sure that for the next customers he visits, my toilet will be the principal protagonist in his monologue.

Sprinklers by Tom

From the dining room window, I watched an older, muddy truck turn into our circular driveway and park in front of the entrance. I rushed to the door, but when I opened it, no one was standing on the covered porch. The truck was still in the driveway.

"I think that the sprinkler guy arrived. Where did he go?" I called my husband.

"I see him walking across the backyard with another fellow. I am sure that he will come in to talk to us," he answered from the living room that looked out on our back lawn and the protected woodland.

Ten minutes later, I met Tom and the young man that accompanied him. He was barely 5'6" high, overweight, with a large protruding stomach, and a face red as a tomato. When he shook my hand, I was surprised to notice his skin felt smooth and without the callouses that someone doing manual work normally would have. He introduced his companion as a helper who was also his son-in-law. The man's physique resembled Tom's. He matched him in height, was heavyset and red in the face. He only didn't share Tom's brown hair. His was ash blond. The similarities between them were so stark that he could have been mistaken for Tom's son. He remained one step behind his father-in-law and did not shake my hand. He kept his course hands with dirt under his fingernails crossed below his belly.

"I am glad that you came because we are having sod put in next week. It will need watering twice a day. At least this is what our landscaper recommended," I explained.

"Did Bruce give you my number?"

"Yes, he did. He highly recommended you."

I continued talking to Tom while my husband disappeared into the kitchen. This was not unusual because he believed that I am a better negotiator in hiring different tradesmen. This type of talk that mixes chatter with business has always bored him.

Bruce described Tom as the best qualified sprinkler installer who would keep our lawn in tip-top condition. He also added that he was from Kentucky, had an eighth-grade education, and spoke with a southern drawl.

"I will install your sprinkler system tomorrow. I walked around your property to calculate the number of heads I need."

His fee for the labor and material was reasonable, and I signed the contract he handed to me.

The following morning both men arrived. I watched Tom's son-in-law unloading from the truck cables, shovels, trench digger machine, sprinkler heads, and other materials and tools with which I was not familiar. Tom stood by giving him directions. He ordered the young man to dig trenches for cables, which was challenging, especially on the sloped backyard. The trench digger machine was heavy and difficult to maneuver through the clay soil. We watched him from the upper deck and heard his heavy breathing and occasional swear words. Tom, on the other hand, did the work that required a knowledge of sprinkler systems. After having installed the buried heads and a switch board in the basement, he programed daily watering of the upcoming sod for a duration of one month and every other day afterwards. In case of rain, the sprinklers would automatically pause. The men finished their work in the late afternoon.

"Call me when the landscapers lay down the sod so that I can adjust the sprinkler heads and replace those that they might damage."

Tom returned the day after the grass was laid on our front and backyard and turned on the sprinkler system. The buried heads sprang up and began scattering water while gyrating.

"When should I call you for shutting off the sprinklers?"

"I usually do it at the end of October. Set up an appointment with my wife. She does bookings for our company."

In the next twenty-two years, I learned about all the happy and sad events in Tom's life. He would tell me about them in April when he would activate our sprinklers and in October when he would winterize them.

"Tom, what do you do during winter when the sprinkler season is over?" I asked him one time.

"We go to Florida inland. I built two houses there, one for my daughter and the other for my wife and me. I love it there. I go fishing in the channels every day."

Whenever Tom mentioned his daughter, his face would light up. She was his only child, a high school graduate who helped run the family business. He never talked about her husband except one time when he bitterly said that if he had not hired him, his son-in-law would be unemployed. I had a feeling that he wished his daughter had married somebody ambitious and industrious instead of that "good-for-nothing" man. It seemed that this was the main reason Tom bossed him around and forced him to do the most physically demanding work required in installing sprinklers.

One April he came alone to open our irrigation system. He had lost a lot of weight, which made him almost unrecognizable.

"How are you, Tom? You look like half of your usual self. What happened?"

"I had a heart attack in February, but I feel okay now. Doctors said that I needed to slim down. I cut portions I used to eat and don't buy fast food anymore. I never drank or smoked cigarettes, so my eating habits were the main culprits."

I found out in October the reason he worked alone.

"I fired that bum because he sided with my wife when she left me. She moved out of our house that I had built in Milford."

"This must have been hard for you."

"It was, but I am angrier than hurt by it. She has no idea that she cannot support herself."

The following April was happier for Tom. His wife returned home, and he described the reasons that made her change her mind about being single again.

"Well, her car broke down, and she had no money to fix it. She was used to having a new car every other year because I bought it for her. She didn't like to go to our cabin up north because the snow needed shoveling, and the fireplace called for logs that she couldn't chop. My daughter and her husband stayed in their warm, rented condominium unwilling to help her. She begged me to take her back. Now everything is normal again, and she is grateful for the lifestyle I provide for her."

"I am glad to hear that your marriage is back on the right track."

A year later, Tom and I exchanged photos of our first grandchildren, chubby little girls. We both were beaming with pride. However, his family bliss did not last long. He and his son-in-law had a falling out and his daughter sided with her husband. They forbade him to see his granddaughter. Not being able to visit the little one devastated him. He was looking forward to taking her fishing in Florida and partaking in her growing up. His daughter and son-in-law stopped working for him. His wife continued answering customers' questions and making appointments on their company's phone.

"They allow my wife to babysit, but I cannot even attend my granddaughter's birthdays," he said angrily. It was clear that this was the most hurtful thing that his family ever put him through.

The last time I saw Tom was in April of 2016, three months before we sold our home and moved to Grand Rapids to be close to our grandchildren. I left his contact number for the new owner together with a glorifying reference. Tom deserved every single word of praise I wrote.

FOUR

The Desert

The car was slowly turning around the curve on the narrow mountain road when the scene in front of Ava's eyes mesmerized her. She gazed at the desert valley that seemed never ending because its furthest limits were covered with a layer of bluish fog. The mountains surrounding it disappeared into gloominess, bypassed by the sunrays on their descent to the valley's surface and creating the illusion of a large lake. She would not have believed that David was driving on a paved road if not for the tumbleweed that began to surface on both sides of it. Ava only saw them in Western movies in scenes when cowboys ride off in haste, leaving behind a cloud of red dust or sand and tumbleweed rolling behind their horses. There was no wind blowing that day, and the tumbleweeds appeared firmly planted in the sand.

"I want to take a couple of pictures of the valley from a distance. Stop the car!" Ava demanded, foreseeing David's resistance.

The car came to a halt, and he unlocked the passenger side door. As Ava began to open it, the scorching heat that burst inside took him by surprise since it surpassed all his pre-existing knowledge of a desert climate.

"Shut the door!" he yelled.

"God dam it! I didn't expect that it would be that hot. What do you think how many degrees?"

"Probably 115 degrees Fahrenheit," Ava calmly replied.

She did not insist on stopping again to take a photo because she wanted to avoid an argument with David that would surely follow. This two-day trip through the desert was supposed to be an adventurous finale to their week-long vacation.

The car continued to slope toward the valley. The asphalted road was the only one that snaked across it. David reluctantly agreed to cross the desert in May, especially after an agent at a tourist agency mentioned that it would be risky travel because of high temperatures and a lack of road assistance in the post-tourist season. The prime time to be in the valley is from January to March. Seeing Ava's enthusiasm for seeing the desert regardless of possible dangers, David didn't want to disappoint her. He loaded the small red rental sedan with gallons of water and bought a detailed map of the valley. For all their earlier trips by land, sea, or air he made sure that they had enough provisions from water to chocolates just in case nothing was available along the way. Ava could not care less about them because the destination itself suppressed all other needs she might have.

The desolate, motionless, extraterrestrial-looking landscape enveloped the car as Ava and David proceeded to drive to the sole motel open for only accidental tourists as they were. The air conditioning inside the sedan was working at its full capacity making their ride pleasant. Their conversation stalled because Ava had an eerie feeling of having been in that desert before, even though she was not quite sure when or why. A sense of familiarity with a place that was supposed to be her first encounter with it puzzled her. She did not share her musing with David because he would dismiss it as nonsensical. He only believed in things that science could prove to be true, and he liked to mock Ava's inkling to give veracity to the scientifically inexplicable. She began to rationalize her feelings of once belonging and living in a dimension far removed from the present. The intense heat did not bother her, the barren terrain of sand dunes and dark mountains that loomed above them did not make her anxious, and the soundless air when she first stepped out of the car filled her with a sense of tranquility and peace. She felt like returning to a place that she once knew well. When they reached the middle of the valley, she insisted on exiting the car whenever she spotted something interesting to photograph or pick up to take along.

"David, stop here. I would like to take a close look at the tumbleweed."

She brought one of them back to take home and placed it in a large clay pot. David watched her behind the closed window of the car thinking:

"She is gently carrying this dried out, unattractive desert plant as if she had an arm full of yellow daffodils from our garden. How can she see any beauty in something so dead? Sometimes I wish I could see what she sees."

"Isn't this plant beautiful, pale gray and completely dry?" Ava asked, smiling. She placed the tumbleweed on the back seat, trying not to break its fragile, miniscule leaves.

Each time Ava ventured out of the car, she came across different sized stones protruding out of the sand. Some of them looked like colored minerals, while others seemed to originate from lava. She collected quite a few of them to give to their friends as a reminder that she thinks of them wherever she goes. The multitude of sand dunes brought Ava great joy. She scaled some of them, and when she reached the top, she waved happily to David, who did not leave the car.

The colors that prevailed in this desert terrain were gold and gray. The absence of green was easily noticed, but Ava knew how the desert was transformed after the rare rainstorm. All those hidden, crawling, walking, and flying creatures would emerge from their hiding places to drink, to bathe, and to wash off the sand and the dust. The indigenous desert plants and flowers would seem to instantly pop up and blossom stroking the valley with a rainbow palette. There would be frantic movement on the ground and in the air. In those times the desert would undergo a metamorphosis from an arid old hag into a young beauty in her best Sunday clothes.

As Ava was sliding down from a sand dune, she felt a shift in the air's idleness into motion. The sudden wind rose from a barely caressing touch to a force that she had to fight in order to reach the car. They were in the eye of a sandstorm, and still miles away from the motel. Ava looked at David and saw him struggling to drive while the visibility diminished in seconds. He unbuttoned a few more buttons on his shirt and rolled up his sleeves up a little bit more, sure signs that he was nervous. The blue cotton shirt he was wearing was soaked with perspiration on the back and under the armpits, and his hair was dripping wet.

"Why are you perspiring so profusely? The air conditioner works just fine," Ava asked him.

"I hate the fact that we came here at the peak of the hottest season and sandstorms. We are the only fools travelling through the desert. Have you seen any cars preceding or following us?" David's frustration and anger came as no surprise to Ann, who was used to his outbursts.

"Are you scared?" Ava asked unruffled by David's fury.

"No, I am not scared. I just don't see a damn thing in front of me because of the sand on the windshield."

The mountains that surrounded the valley became shadows behind the avalanche of sand. On clear days, they attract tourists because of their different colors caused by minerals that form them. On that day, however, the sandstorm blocked the narrow road passage through them. In addition to frequent sand and dust storms, a unique property of the valley was its geographical position. It was the lowest elevation on the continent and below sea level. Ava and David guessed that this might be the reason why they could not find any radio frequency for listening to music.

"Ava, this is really creepy. I feel like I'm being cut off from the outside world."

"I don't feel like you do. We are in the natural world, no distractions, no escape from oneself, just an assimilation of sensations."

The sandstorm cleared up as fast as it came in, and calm was restored. David had to brush off the sand from the car, and some that entered inside. They resumed their drive. On the top of a small hill, not far from the road, they saw a plaque indicating the remnants of an old borax mine. Ava suggested that they investigate it. David reluctantly agreed. She walked in front of him and watched her feet not to step on poisonous desert crawlers and insects. Not seeing any, she concluded that they must be hiding somewhere and would come out only in the night when there was no danger of being burned to ashes by the sun. It was early afternoon, and the sun was still high. When she reached the mine, she noticed that the rubber soles of her espadrilles began to stick to the asphalt. She looked at the bottom of one of them and saw that it had partly melted. They were disappointed that the only remains of the mine were an old wooden wagon in front of the entrance.

"It must have been awful working in here," David said.

"No worse than in any other mine," Ava replied because she was convinced that any labor done underground must feel like being buried alive.

Once they returned to the car David looked around and commented:

"I always imagined the Moon's surface looking like this, but with less sand."

"You are right. It does feel like being on another planet. Well, to tell you the truth, I always knew how a desert looks," Ava replied as a matter of fact.

"How could you know?" he asked, amused.

"You have never been in any desert before. Perhaps you saw it on *National Geographic*?"

"I lived in a desert in one of my previous lives. I'm sure of it. Can't you see? I can stand the heat without sweating. I didn't drink anything so far, while you finished two gallons of water. How do you explain that?" Ava challenged him, hoping for an original answer.

"This is just the dumbest thing I ever heard. Are you in your belief in the reincarnation phase again?" he asked sarcastically.

"He always says everything is stupid that he doesn't understand, and I have an explanation for it," Ava thought.

The sensation of complete comfort and ease and the closeness to the vast emptiness of the desert filled her with a sense of security, as she wondered who or what she might have been at one point in time.

David and Ava had spent many good years together regardless of their contrasting characters. He always knew what he wanted, liked, and disliked, and she was seldom sure about anything. He hardly ever changed his mind, and she was always absorbed by new ideas and willing to forgo her old ones. She had never gotten used to his lack of imagination and persistent inertia. This was just a parenthesis in their partnership because his integrity, honesty, and devotion to her made up for his shortcomings. Despite her at times flamboyant nature, and a lack of interest and knowledge in subjects dear to David, he considered Ava his intellectual equal. They fought with gusto clashing over issues that each of them held essential to their well-being such as financial matters, extended family dynamics, and household chores. Even in the heat of an argument, they did hear each other out because they cared what the other had to say.

After six hours of driving, they finally reached the motel. To their surprise, it was located in an oasis nested among short trees with large crowns. The grounds also had several bungalows, a few houses for employees, a restaurant, a small museum, and a pool. The receptionist told them that they are at capacity in the winter months when day temperatures dip into the mid-60's, and people come for horseback riding and hiking.

Once situated in their room, Ava and David wanted to visit the museum sitting on one side of the large grass-covered lawn. A dwarfed tree planted at the entrance had a crow sitting motionless on it. The bird was covered with shiny black fathers and its human-like eyes looked straight at Ava paying no attention to David. She felt uneasy but decided to return the crow's gaze. Their eyes met, and Ava said quietly, "Hello," first letting David enter the museum so as not to hear her greeting. He would certainly think that she was out of her mind. The crow answered in a clear human voice:

"Hello. You are back!"

"You know me?" Ava asked surprised.

"I do. I recognized your voice. It's still the same, kind of high-pitched. You look different though. You are a woman. When I met you, you were not human."

"Who was I? Tell me, please!" Ava begged.

"You were a fish, a tiny, red fish."

"How could I be a fish in the desert? It doesn't make any sense."

"Do you see a small pond by those date trees? This has been the only water in the whole valley for a very long time. It is the place where I saw you for the first time, jumping happily out of the water and diving back into it. You were always so playful, eager to meet other fish swimming with you, as well as creatures that came to drink from the pond. I remember you inviting me to join you, but I couldn't because I didn't know how to swim. You tried to fly then, but you didn't go further than the length of your body extended out of the water. Afterwards we decided just to talk. We became friends."

"Did we talk every day?" Ava wanted to know.

"Almost every day. Sometimes I didn't make it back in time from my food-searching trips, and you would already be asleep. I would wait for you to wake up at dawn, and then we would tell each other what we did the previous day."

"We were really good friends, weren't we?" Ava tried to jog her memory.

"Oh yes, we were. Then one day you just disappeared, and I didn't see you anymore. I looked for you every day, sat next to the pond night after night hoping that you would suddenly splash me with your leaps out of the water. But you vanished, without a trace. I gave up hope and didn't look for you anymore. Later the people diverted part of the water from the pond and filled the pool with it."

Ava looked at the date trees and remembered seeing them daily. She walked to a larger puddle that was once a pond and tasted the water. It was sweet and its flavor was familiar.

"How old are you?" Ava asked the crow.

"As old as you are--hundreds of years. Thank you for the memories, whoever you are now."

The crow flew away without having anything else to say.

Ava and David returned to their room. Their luggage was unpacked, and they had no other plans as to how to spend what was left of that day. They felt like swimming because it seemed like an improbable luxury in a desert. The pool's existence was somehow bizarre and yet explicable. It was filled with water from the pond that sustained life thousands of years before man's arrival. Ava saw the pool as a metaphor for life. Clad in their bathing suits, they slid into the water. It was warmer than expected. They swam for an hour, and when they came out, they noticed that their bathing suits were bone dry by the time they reached the lounge chairs. The hot air had absorbed all the moisture out of them.

There were two other guests lounging at the pool. Ava and David introduced themselves, and asked the first one:

"Is this your first time here?"

"No, to answer your question. I end up here every winter because I like to recite Shakespeare when nobody is around. By the way, I am Chuck."

His reply was unexpected, and the only comment they could think of was noncommittal:

"How interesting."

The other pool visitor, Samuel, after introducing himself, proceeded to describe his drunken days in Paris as a young man. His story made perfect sense because his slurred speech and a half empty bottle of whisky next to his lounge chair confirmed the truthfulness of his monologue. Both were bizarre characters attracted to the valley for some obscure personal reason.

Ava and David left the pool at nightfall. She bought a bottle of Prosecco at the bar and proposed that they drink it on the lawn behind their room. They were tired from the trip and swimming and abandoned themselves in plastic patio chairs. Ava sipped the bubbly liquid that was slowly overtaking her. David finished his first glass in one gulp and didn't continue drinking. They both looked at the night sky full of stars. There were so many of them, and they appeared to be closer to the earth than usual. Ava imagined them falling on her and David as if thrown out of a large basket. Their clear view of the stars was suddenly interrupted by thousands of bats flying frantically out of the trees and from the rooftops as if looking for new lodging somewhere high in the sky. They were everywhere, and some of them circled close to Ava's head, which frightened her. All of a sudden Ava heard the roaring sound of tumbling water, something like a gigantic sea wave rolling over mountain peaks.

"Damn, I knew this might happen. We are below sea level. The sea will flow over us!" she concluded.

"David, do you hear anything?"

"No. Just the air conditioning running," he replied calmly, continuing to doze off.

"Lucky man!" she thought. "He never feels anything coming. And when it does, what's he going to do? He's totally unprepared for any change."

"I know what I'm going to do. I'll swim. A fish ought to swim. A bird ought to fly. A man has to figure it out. He's always given too many choices."

My Smith-Corona

At first, I did not realize what a wonderful thing a typewriter could be until I got a fancy one, the latest model, and an electronic one with a built-in word processor. It was an anniversary gift from my husband, and being too practical to excite me, I rejected it instantly. I am the world's worse typist and surely the slowest one because I type only with my forefinger. I could never make a living as a secretary or in any other profession which requires a lot of typing because I belong to a pre-computer generation whose school curricula did not include this practical skill. However, I could probably learn it if I really needed to. I truly envy people who can type without looking at the keyboard and simultaneously employ both hands.

I owned an old model of a Smith-Corona for ten years. I became fond of it because I got to know its shortcomings and learned how to fix its technical problems. For example, I continued to rewind the ribbon manually because I could not figure out how to do it automatically. I convinced myself that my way was the only possible one and blamed the typewriter for its imperfection. I also faulted it for producing the uppercase letters slightly elevated from the line on which the lowercase ones stood, thus making my typed texts look sloppy. Thankfully, I did not have to do a lot of typing at that time, and my old Corona satisfied my needs. The two of us developed a friendship based on our mutual predictability and flaws. My loyalty to the old typewriter caused me to hate its youngest cousin that was sophisticated, unpredictable, and smart.

At first, I refused even to open the new Smith-Corona. I let it sit on my desk for several weeks and purposely misplaced the manual that explained how to operate it. The search for it was my excuse for not being able to use the typewriter. My husband was offended by my ignoring his gift and by my persistence in continuing typing on my dear old Corona.

"You have been just stubborn. I'll show you how the new typewriter works, and you will see how simple it is."

One evening I finally gave up and decided to appease him. I found myself in front of a light gray, sleekly designed typewriter with my husband hovering over me and explaining, according to him, just a few differences between my old Corona and this new one. His lengthy clarification bored me to tears. He expected me to memorize all the advanced properties of the new typewriter such as the computerized margins, the automatic correction of a single letter or the whole word, underlining, bold print, italics, capitalization of titles, five pages of memory, a corrective vocabulary with 50,000 words, accent marks found in foreign languages, and the list goes on.

"Could you please just show me how to put the paper in, and I'll continue on my own," I said impatiently.

"That's easy, let me show you," he replied pleased with my willingness to begin to use his gift. He reached for two pounds of professional typing paper. I watched his disappointment when his first attempt to insert one sheet failed. I must have had a victory expression on my face when that paper came out all wrinkled because he threw it on the floor angrily. Several others met the same fate, and the pile of crumpled sheets grew. I began to enjoy myself watching him getting frustrated over his failed tries.

"If you don't want to use it, don't! But you are really stupid!" He screamed at me and stormed out of the room.

He blamed my negative attitude toward the new Corona for his inability to accomplish the very first, simplest step in using it.

"I didn't say that I don't want to give it a try," I yelled after him.

Well, I knew it. All these fancy, complicated gadgets are so pretentious I hate them, was my conclusion. I got up and turned my back on the typewriter, ready to leave. Suddenly I felt the jolt of a challenge. I grabbed a new sheet, placed it precisely at the left end of the roller, and pressed the code "Insert." The paper smoothly slid under the roller, as straight as it could be, and it stared at me in expectation that I would fill its empty white surface with some typed content.

"Fuck you!" I demonstrably said, turning off the Corona. I closed its cover and shoved it under my desk.

My husband refused to talk to me over the following few days, and I ignored his gift but not completely. I thought of using the Corona's attachment as a word processor, which could make my job-related tasks less stressful. As a university lecturer, I have to type students' tests, midterms, and final exams, as well as recommendations. I do not mind teaching every day, but what I really enjoy is writing fiction. I have been doing it for several years. Writing became both my emotional outlet and a refuge from the grinding hustle and bustle of my daily routine. I shut the door of our bedroom, sit at my desk, and handwrite on a lined yellow pad. The silence around me lets my inside world speak. I think of those few hours of solitude as sacred and only mine. Nothing compares to the satisfaction I get by seeing words flowing out of my pen and freeing my emotions. I feel purified and renewed. My husband does not understand that I cannot be creative while I type because I am focusing on the mechanics of the typewriter. The noise that comes from my pressing on the keyboard causes me to lose my concentration. I need silence, my yellow pad with lines, and the black pen, things that the Corona makes obsolete.

"You could type what you have handwritten and revise it by using the word processor," my husband suggested breaking the status quo.

"He really wants me to use the damn typewriter," I thought.

I finally surrendered to my husband's wishes. I lovingly placed my old Corona in her black, scratched, heavy plastic casing and stored it in the back of my closet. I had to face the new Smith-Corona for the second time. I was determined to learn everything about her quickly in order to be able to control her. My resentment of her turned into a challenge to make her pliable to my wishes. I angrily inserted the first sheet, and the Corona processed it. I stared at the white paper not knowing what to write. My mind went blank. After a few seconds, I looked at the miniature screen above the keypads and read a sentence that she wrote: "I am thinking." I had to smile because she broke the ice to facilitate our future communication. I accepted her peace offering.

"Do you know what I am thinking about?" I asked her.

"Still thinking," she wrote back.

When my right-hand forefinger touched one letter on the Corona's keypad, the words, "Still thinking," disappeared. She knew that her role was to type words, and mine was to produce them.

"Corona, the one thing I really want is that one day somebody will enjoy reading what I wrote," I typed.

She did not comment.

"I am failing to communicate with my husband. He has gradually drifted away from me," I typed.

Her silence persisted.

"Do you think that it is entirely my fault?"

"Error!" she typed back.

"You mean I did everything I could to make our marriage work better?"

"Error!" she repeated.

"What was I supposed to do? I was interested in his work, in his thoughts; I tried to share myself with him. I was loyal. Do you think I am boring and ordinary? Do I nag too much?"

"Error!" typed again.

"Thank you! I have such low esteem lately. The loneliness is killing me. Do you ever feel lonely?"

Tack, tack, tack. The keys on the keypad jumped up and down without me touching them.

"I guess not. Typewriters must not get lonely, just rusty. But people get rusty too. Do you think that I am rusty?"

Tack, tack, tack.

"No opinion! How come? Oh, please don't shut me off!"

Tack, tack, tack.

"I really hate being ignored. Stop doing it! I am getting angry!"

"Margin error!" came the typed comment.

"You are absolutely right. My margins are too small, and getting narrower, because my husband wants me in his margins, and I just cannot squeeze myself to fit in them anymore. Self-imposed rigid margins of one's existence erase any ability to evolve, to become open to new experiences, to embrace the unpredictable, and to live with imperfections. Space and time have their margins, and sometimes they coincide. What do you think?"

Tack, tack, tack.

"I see. You do not have an opinion. I believe that my spatial and temporal margins existed even before my conception. I drag them with me wherever I am and only lose them when I write. I feel as boundless and free as a cordless kite or balloon. This sensation of flying up high in the sky is so liberating and wonderful! What do you say?"

Tack, tack, tack.

"I know that you are stationary, desk-bound, but I am sure that you understand what I am talking about. Do you have any advice about how I can better my life? What should I do? Speak up! I am listening."

"Error at the beginning." Correct!

 "Leads to more errors!" Correct!

I hate intelligent machines. They know how to outsmart you.

Feathered Fear

My wife, Gina, is the only person I know who fears all birds, from colorful exotic ones to those that inhabit trees in our backyard, to the entire family of poultry. I discovered this phobia of hers in the first few months of our marriage. One lazy Sunday afternoon in May we visited the well-known zoo in Toledo, where we lived at that time. After strolling by the lions' den and watching the tigers sleeping in their cage, we entered the monkey house, which smelled so badly that I suggested:

"Let's go out! I need some fresh air. How about if we see parrots? They are nearby in their outdoor cages."

Gina pulled her hand out of mine and said firmly: "I am not interested in birds. I want to see giraffes."

I didn't understand her refusal but didn't pay too much attention to it, and I didn't ask her why she didn't want to see the parrots. This was just the first of many incidents in which Gina distanced herself from observing birds both in zoos and in city parks, their natural habitat. She also refused to cross several Toledo streets because pigeons gathered there looking for crumbs. On our first trip to Venice, she was horrified seeing tourists feeding hundreds of pigeons and taking selfies with one or more of them sitting on their shoulders and heads. Initially I could not understand her aversion toward these harmless creatures, but throughout the years, I learned that it was useless trying to change her feelings. The only explanation she would give me was:

"I don't like them."

Last Saturday we were invited for dinner at the home of a newly hired business associate of mine, Jack Strong. Gina spent half the afternoon getting ready for our rare outing. She even colored her red-toned hair to cover the gray strands on her temples, not because she wants to hide her age, but because she doesn't want to look unkempt. Appearances have always been important to her. She believes that the way she presents herself to the world mirrors the harmony between her mind and her surroundings, primarily our home. Gina's neatness regarding the organization of our household borders on obsession. Her striving for perfection in all things she considers being under her domain makes her neatly fold her towels on the towel rack after each shower, organizing her clothes according to seasons and continuing to sub-organize them by colors. The plastic box with her sewing items – threads, needles, and other gadgets – follows the order of frequency of their use. Everything in our house is labeled and has its designated place, mostly known only to her. I don't even bother looking for an item that I need because it's so much easier for her to bring it to me.

I got dressed and came to the hallway to pick up the car keys from a small glass console, when Gina appeared wearing a black pencil skirt, white blouse, and wrapped in a black shawl. She was dressed for a festive occasion. She took one look at me and asked:

"You are going dressed like this?" She could not hide her anger.

"What's wrong with it?" I asked, pretending not to know. I did not want to irritate her. I just tried to bypass her inspection of my attire. I prefer my comfort to a formal dress code.

"You cannot wear a T-shirt under your jacket. You need a shirt and a tie," she commanded.

I reluctantly agreed to the shirt but refused the tie.

Once we sat in the car, Gina's anger subsided. She was looking forward to an entertaining evening. We arrived on time, thanks to her telling me that the dinner was half an hour earlier than I remember being written in the invitation. It is one of her tricks to make sure that we are not the last to arrive, which she considers being rude and inconsiderate to hosts. The hostess, Mrs. Strong, opened the door and greeted us with a broad smile and a warm "Hello" and "Welcome." She led us to a large living room where several of the early guests were already enjoying their drinks and appetizers. While she was introducing us, her husband got up from the sofa to greet us. He was a tall, imposing figure in his early fifties, sure of himself and obviously proud of what he had accomplished in life. Our introduction interrupted the mingling of the guests for a few minutes, but they resumed their small group chatting without paying any further attention to us. I knew most of the men from the office, and some of their wives. Gina, being a master small talk conversationalist, began to mix with ease among the people she knew and with those she just met holding a glass of white wine in her left hand and balancing a small plate with horse d' oeuvres on her right. In our later commentaries of the dinner, we both agreed that our hosts had put forth an extra effort to make us feel comfortable and welcome us in their stately home since this was our first visit.

Mrs. Strong was a slender, elegant woman in her forties who obviously spent a lot of time in different spas and sport clubs judging from her sporty physique. We found out in the course of the evening that she and her husband belong to the local country club where they often play golf and dine on filet mignon and lobster afterward. While the other guests were arriving, Mrs. Stone quickly introduced them and continued to glide gracefully from one group of guests to the other exchanging pleasantries. She was not interested either in details of their lives nor their opinions on a particular subject. Politics and religion were off the table because they could arouse controversies and ruin the lightness of the air at the party.

After an hour of the guests' chitchat, Mrs. Strong gently prodded us to go to a formal dining room where the dinner would be served. Twelve of us sat at the designated chairs in the formation of altering man-woman seating. We all admired the long cherry wood Queen Ann table topped with the embroidered place settings, fine China plates of different sizes, sterling silver silverware, monogrammed white napkins, and two short vases filled with daffodils in the middle. Several lit candles placed in between the vases created an intimate atmosphere when the crystal chandelier's light was dimmed. We began to converse with people sitting next to us while the hostess with the help of her husband brought in the first course - a tomato soup. The entrée included mashed potatoes, green beans, and a mixed greens salad. Her husband came into the dining room ceremoniously carrying a roasted capon on a large silver platter. He had this huge smile on his face when he began to carve the plumb bird at the loud "aha" and "oho" of his guests.

"Voila!" he said, pleased with his carving technique done in about five minutes.

I glanced at my wife and saw that her enthusiasm for the meal abruptly vanished. She tried to hide it with a polite smile. This was nothing new to me. A dinner with poultry as the main dish for her is a culinary failure. For this reason, our close friends never invite us for southern fried chicken, chestnut-stuffed turkey, roasted duck, or Cornish hens. Most people, though, consider poultry a safe choice and serve it when they have guests for dinner for the first time.

"Everybody likes chicken" is a phrase that gained popularity years ago.

"Not my wife," I was thinking.

As the hostess passed the food around the table, I watched Gina filling up her plate with potatoes, a tiny piece of capon next to them, beans, and a salad on a salad plate. She ate everything, except the capon. She praised the dinner and was relieved that nobody seemed to notice that she did not touch the meat. I am surprised that so far, she had never said at the beginning of these "insignificant meals" (her description) that she is a vegetarian as she from time to time threatens to do in the future. I know she will not do it because she would never purposely hurt anyone's feelings.

Gina is a very health-conscious person, and one day of each week she faithfully prepares one poultry-based dinner for me and our children.

"You should not eat red meat and pork all the time," she is fond of saying as she takes those roasted to a crisp Cornish hens or chicken out of the oven.

"It's bad for your cholesterol. Poultry is very healthy and cheaper than other meats, which is important these days."

Her health argument always has a twist of justification and almost an apology attached to it because she continues to serve poultry in spite of our preference for beef and pork.

"It's in your best interest, and I will continue making it."

Our poultry day is her pork chops day. She fries two large pork chops and eats them with a mouth-watering gusto, never mentioning the cholesterol or other health hazards that befall those who eat fatty meats. Over time, we ended up liking chicken Marsala and duck stuffed with apples, and we therefore overlooked her double standards.

Gina had a valid explanation for her attitude concerning all feather-covered creatures. I think that she actually had a full-blown ornithophobia. She told us that when she was four or five years old and lived in the former Yugoslavia, she used to play with the children from the apartment above that of her parents'. Their father was an alcoholic and a professional motorcycle racer who was always dressed in black leather pants and jacket even when he was not competing. He was frequently drunk even a few hours before a major race. In order to sober him up as fast as possible, his wife would give him a cup of strong coffee in which she would put ashes from the wood burning stove. She believed that the ashes stopped the alcohol from circulating into his brain. Gina was convinced that this was true because the man never crashed and killed himself or others while racing. His extended family lived on a farm outside of the city and would bring him several large hens at a time to help him feed his children. In the early fifties, the post-war years, her country and many other European ones lived through rations, which allowed a weekly purchase of one kilogram of meat per family. These hens, kept in a large wooden cage on their balcony, and the produce from the farm enabled his family to survive, considering that not winning the race meant no earnings.

One day Gina was playing hide and seek with the man's children in their apartment. As a prank, the older boy put one of the hens on her head while she was facing the wall and counting up to twenty while the others were supposed to hide. She had long, curly hair, and the bird got its feet tangled in it. It tried to free itself by jumping on her head, flapping its wings, and cackling. Gina screamed, terrified. The children laughed hysterically finding her panic amusing. The hen stayed on her head until her mother heard her screams, rushed up the flight of stairs, opened the unlocked door of the apartment, and put the hen into her cage. For a month after that incident, Gina would wake up in the night, sit in her bed, and cry.

This incident alone would have been enough to cause her ornithophobia, but one more equally terrifying cemented it. The description of it calls for some context. Gina's aunts who lived on a farm used to bring chickens and hens to her mother in exchange for hers, my father's, and my used clothes. They were not the only ones partaking in that postwar economy. At that time, the country's textile industry production was limited in quantity and did not offer any variety of styles and fabrics. The city people wore what they had saved from the years before the war. The farmers knew that, and rather than selling their poultry and produce on the open market, they preferred going door to door in major cities. Getting money for their products was useless because most of the stores were semi-empty. At the beginning of their business enterprise, they would ask just for a pair of old shoes, slacks, or a shirt, but as the demand for chickens and hens grew, they bargained for a good coat, a woolen dress, or a suit for a single chicken. Gina's mother appreciated it when her sisters brought the farm goods and always had a bag of old clothes waiting for them. However, she never knew what kind of clothing they needed and the quantity they expected to get. That frustrated her, causing tension between them.

Sometimes Gina's aunts would bring the chickens already butchered, and other times they brought them alive in case they were too small and needed to grow more before slaughtering. Gina's mother would keep them in a wooden cage on the balcony, the same kind as the upstairs neighbors had. She would put the corn at the bottom of the cage and watch them fighting over each kernel. When they reached the desirable size, she would slaughter them and prepare them for roasting.

My wife's description of the killing of two particular chickens still haunts me.

"One Sunday morning my mother decided to kill two chickens and prepare them for lunch. I was watching the killing from the balcony. She stood in the middle of the kitchen with a metal plate in front of her feet that was supposed to collect the blood dripping from the slit neck of the first chicken. She squeezed the bird between her ankles to immobilize it. The chicken's cackle turned into a piercing sound of a creature that felt its imminent end. I covered my ears with my hands and continued watching my mother holding the chicken's head with one hand and exposing its neck. She began to cut the neck with a large knife. The blood splattered across her legs. The bird stopped fighting and was motionless. My mother was sure that it was dead, so she placed it on the floor next to the plate and was getting the other chicken from the cage. To the horror of both of us, the chicken got up from the floor, began to run frenetically through the kitchen with its head wobbling on the half-severed neck. It stepped once into the plate full of its own blood, and by flapping in circles, it left the bloody tracks behind. My mother screamed and called my father for help to catch the chicken and finish it off. I guess she just could not stand it any longer. Her hands were covered in blood, and I felt like throwing up. She later told her sisters not to bring live chickens anymore. From that time on my aunts would only bring chickens and hens already dead."

However, my wife also remembers the arrival of those birds and the treatment they received in her mother's kitchen.

"My aunts would bring them still covered with feathers that needed to be plucked. My mother would place them in a large pot and throw boiling water over them to loosen the feathers. The whole kitchen would reek of those steaming feathers. She would pluck almost all of them and the remaining small ones would burn off with a lighter. At the end, the chickens appeared naked, and their yellowish skin disgusted me. My mother would throw the feathers from the chickens and hens in the garbage, but those of the geese she saved for stuffing pillows. We would get one young goose each Christmas."

The thing is that Gina does not feel just disgust for chickens, hens, ducks, geese, and the like - she is afraid of them. One summer we visited her cousin, Mara, on the farm ten miles away from Toledo. We wanted the children to spend a day outdoors breathing the unpolluted air and playing with their cousins. At lunchtime we all sat at a large wooden table in front of Mara's house ready to eat homemade corn bread and in-house smoked ham. Her dog and several cats circled the table hoping to get some treats from us. We all resisted at Mara's urging because they were already fat. Chickens and hens were roaming around us as well, accompanied by four white geese. Gina said that she preferred to eat inside, in the cool family room whose window overlooked the table; thus, she would not be far from the rest of us. Supposedly the heat of the noon sun bothered her, but I knew the real reason. She was in a state of panic to be attacked by one of those huge geese.

Gina acknowledges the beauty of some exotic birds with their colorful feathers, and she does not mind the sound of birds chirping coming from the woods behind our house, but she insisted that I remove a blue jay's nest from one of our gutters. We even have a birdhouse hanging on the dogwood near our garage. She puts in birdseed for the native birds and invites our children to watch them flying in to feed; she wants to teach them to appreciate nature. She was once even a bird-sitter for a myna bird while our friends were vacationing. The bird would greet her with "hello" every time she would come to feed it. One time the bird hissed at her, and she threatened it by saying that she would not replenish its food and water dish. After that the bird would hide in one corner of the cage at feeding time, probably more scared of my wife than dying from thirst and hunger. They both suffered from a phobia of each other.

I never realized what torture it must have been for my wife when we lived with my parents for a couple of months after we got married. They had a small, talking parakeet called Greg who was allowed to fly throughout the house during the day. Gina was pregnant with our son at that time. When she was home, she used to wear a quilted pink robe with a large floral print on it. Greg was attracted to that robe, and whenever Gina would iron in the kitchen, he would immediately land on her shoulder close to her ear. As a newcomer in our family, she didn't want to make an issue of her phobia, so she never requested that the bird be caged. During the night Greg slept on the balcony in his cloth-covered cage. One night there was a big storm with a lot of lightning. Greg got scared and flew frantically around the cage. He hit the top of the cage and fractured his skull. The next morning, we found him lying dead at the bottom of his cage. Everyone was heartbroken, but Gina did not partake in our mourning. I swear that I noticed a quick smile of relief on her face, but she quickly wiped it away so as not to be labeled as cruel.

The dinner at the Strongs was almost over. The conversation at the table was slowly heading toward its closure when someone introduced an unexpected subject of reincarnation. Most of the people were caught by surprise but became quickly animated. Some of the gests did not believe in it; others were intrigued, but one man said firmly:

"When I die, I am going to return as a bird."

"How terrible! I couldn't stand nor could I ever trust anybody that walks this earth covered in feathers. You would never be my friend," Gina could not resist replying.

Everyone laughed, my wife included, but I knew that she meant every word she said. Gina is convinced that she will return as a fish.

Last Cigarette

I quickly passed my irreplaceable forty-year-old comb through my hair. If I ever lost it, I would be very unhappy because no other one could be that suitable for my thick, curly hair. By now it is a bit bent, but its functionality is still perfect. I am one of those people with an irrational attachment to objects that others would toss in the garbage bin. I rushed downstairs from the second-floor bathroom to join my husband in his rare shopping at the Twelve Oaks Mall. He wanted to buy some comfortable summer shorts. Since I didn't see him in the kitchen, I guessed that he must have been cooling his KIA that was parked for several days in the 90-degree Fahrenheit garage.

"I'll be out in a second. Let me put some lipstick on," I yelled from the powder room near the garage.

As I was taking the last look at myself in the mirror, I realized that his car was not running. *Maybe he pulled out of the garage and is waiting for me in the car*, I thought. I opened the entrance hall door and found him sitting on the stairs landing, smoking a cigarette.

"Why are you sitting here?"

I asked him calmly because this image of him struck me as odd. He could have been smoking in the kitchen because I had stopped complaining about the awful smell that his two packs a day of Kents emitted and dispersed throughout the first floor of our house. I nagged him about it for years, until I finally accepted the obvious fact that he was neither going to puff away outdoors nor quit smoking for good.

"I don't feel well. I think that I am having a heart attack. Drive me to the Providence ER," he answered in a composed tone of voice.

I didn't ask him to elaborate on his self-diagnosis because being an MD, I knew that he was right. His face was pale, and the sweat covered his forehead signaling that he was in pain. He held an almost finished cigarette in his right hand. Its ashes formed a small pile on the step below. I dashed to my Honda and opened the passenger side door for him. He got in and slumped on the seat. As I pressed on the accelerator pedal, an eerie calm engulfed my mind. I became aware that it was imperative that I reach the ER as soon as possible. I had a task in front of me and drove above the speed limit. The four-mile drive seemed like a never-ending distance. The thought that my husband might not survive a heart attack never entered my consciousness. I felt like my brain could only focus on that single mission of driving fast.

"My pain is in my wrists now," was the first sentence he said.

We finally arrived at the hospital. He got out of the car without waiting for me to grab my purse and shut off the engine. When I reached him in the lobby, he was already describing his symptoms to the receptionist. I gave her our insurance card. The following sequence of events left me in a state of numbness as if my mind and body could not process what was going on around me.

Two patient transporters wheeled my husband into a small, curtain enclosed cubicle with an exam bed and a monitor. There was also a chair for the person who accompanied the patient. An ER doctor asked my husband to describe his pain on the scale of 1-10. It was 8. He confirmed his self-diagnosis and told him that the ambulance would take him to downtown Providence where the medical team was going to wait for him and open his blocked heart vessels. The doctor was looking at numbers on the monitor that measured my husband's vital signs. He gave him a shot of morphine to relieve his pain. After that, he addressed me for the first time.

"You are the wife, right? You can ride in the ambulance if you wish or follow it."

I just nodded as a sign that I understood. I am sure that he had witnessed many spouses in my position who cried or became hysterical from fear of losing their partners causing them to fail to hear his directions. My husband was placed in an advanced life support ambulance along with a paramedic who continued to check his vital signs during the transfer. I sat next to a heavyset driver who didn't waste any time driving out of the hospital grounds. He pressed on the gas pedal and turned on the siren. I'll never forget that thirty-mile ride on highway 96. The driver zigzagged in and out of the lanes and the speedometer showed 90 mph. It was obvious that it was not his first race to save somebody's life that was hanging on a thread. His concentration was at the highest point. Both of us kept quiet. I turned around hoping to see my husband through a small window that separated the cab from the patient compartment. Instead, I saw the paramedic lifting his thumb as a sign that my husband was stable. With brakes squealing the driver stopped at the hospital's rear entrance where a group of nurses was already waiting for the ambulance's arrival. I only had a second to look at my husband's face before they rushed him to the operating room. He seemed placid and his eyes were closed as if he were sleeping. Clearly morphine had taken effect.

"There is a waiting room close to the operating room. You can wait there," one of the nurses told me in a gentle, comforting voice. She probably noticed a bewildered look on my face and that I had accompanied my husband alone. Such life-threatening events usually involve the entire family in support. As soon as I entered the relatives' room, I saw a large group of people of different ages that I remembered from the ER lobby forty minutes ago. They entered shortly after my husband and me. They pushed a wheelchair with a man in his late forties. I overheard them telling the receptionist that he collapsed in his garage. The symptoms that they described were identical to my husband's. They talked in hushed voices, hugging, and comforting each other. Nobody prayed, which surprised me.

I have to call the kids and tell them what is going on, I decided.

When I retrieved the cell phone out of my large, always messy purse, I saw that it had run out of charge, nothing unusual in my taking care of it. My husband used to remind me to charge it in the evening and have it at 100% before driving to work. I didn't want to ask anyone from the group to let me use his or her cellphone because I knew that my request would intrude on their tight unity of intense emotions. Instead, I stopped a passing nurse and asked her if there was a phone available to visitors.

"You can use this one on the counter, just dial 0 before your number."

I first called our son. I described to him what was going on with his father. Being an MD himself, he had many medical questions that I tried to answer the best that I could. He wanted to know all the details, some of which became foggy in my head. His voice was calm, unemotional. He didn't utter any words of reassurance that his dad would be OK, nor did he ask me how I was feeling. Perhaps he was more aware of the gravity of the situation than I was, which made him sound cold and uncaring.

"Call your sister. I am on the hospital's landline phone, and I am not sure I am able to make a long-distance call. I'll keep in touch."

I hung up the phone and looked at the other family members still standing in a circle and waiting for an update on their relative's condition. He was in the second operating room. Suddenly, I felt all alone with no one to comfort me and ease my anxiety. I remained frozen next to the white telephone as if waiting for a call from the great one above telling me that my husband would live. The nurse that emerged from the first operating room walked toward me with a smile on her face:

"Your husband is OK. You can visit him in ICU on the third floor in 30 minutes."

"Thank you," was the only thing I was able to say. The tears flooded my face. She briefly hugged me. Hers was the first consoling gesture that made me feel that I mattered, that she understood what I was going through.

I called our son again to give him the happy news. He said that his sister became hysterical when he told her what happened that morning. Her reaction didn't surprise me. The bond between her dad and her was always strong. They understood each other from early on. She valued his opinion and often accepted his advice on matters in which she had needed an outsider's input. Half an hour passed, and I pressed button #3 in the elevator. My husband's room was on the right, number

364. The humming sound of various medical machines came out of several rooms with open doors and the odor of disinfectant permeated the entire space. As I was looking at the room numbers, I saw a priest exiting the one I was approaching. I froze, unable to move forward.

They told me that he was OK. Why was the priest in his room? He is not religious. Do they send the clergy for last rites because it's a Catholic hospital? Is he dead? Questions were racing through my mind.

The priest zoomed by me, and only then I realized that he came out of room 365. I tried to be composed as I entered my husband's room. He looked exhausted and lay motionless in his bed. He was in a horizontal position without a pillow under his head.

"Come on in! I am OK. I have to lie completely still until my artery closes and the blood coagulates. I am in no pain," he clarified his position. "The cardiologist who worked on me will come shortly to explain to you what they did," he said with a tired smile on his face.

"Hello, how is my patient?" the cardiologist cheerfully asked.

"Thank you, doctor. I feel OK except it is hard to lie completely still on my back. This is my wife, Romana."

"By the evening, we will remove the sandbag, and you will be able to eat your dinner."

"Let me show both of you what I did today."

The doctor opened a white legal pad and drew the image of the heart with the surrounding blood vessels and the aorta. He marked with an ex the vein that was 100% closed in which he inserted a stent. He also pointed out another one that was 90% blocked which he wanted to open the following Tuesday.

"You can take your husband home on Wednesday, but I am not done yet. He has to come back after a week because he needs a third stent."

At this point, he referred only to me as if my husband were no longer in the room. I understood, he counted on me to monitor his patient's reaction to the present stent and the future ones.

"No smoking cigarettes ever again!" His stern warning came with a smile to lessen the impact of it, knowing how hard it was going to be for my husband to abstain from lighting at least one Kent.

"The nurse is on her way to put a nicotine patch on your arm. I'll see you tomorrow."

The nurse was a chubby young man and, with a grin told, my husband, "This patch will make you happy. What would you like to eat for dinner?"

"What do you recommend?" My husband wanted to know because his own patients often complained about the bland hospital food.

"The steak and mashed potatoes are the best."

I was surprised by his answer and expected that he would suggest a vegetarian meal more suitable for a recent stent recipient. The other thought that crossed my mind was that he perhaps entertained the notion that this dinner could be my husband's last, so why not make him doubly happy—a patch and a good dinner for an overweight older man.

I stayed with my husband for two hours when he told me that I should go home because he felt OK, and I needed to decompress. He saw the worried look on my face.

"I left my car in the Providence parking lot. I'll call a cab."

I kissed my husband on his forehead and took one last look at the room to make sure that he had everything he needed in case of an emergency. There was a monitor connected with the front desk for showing sudden heart related distress; the portable toilet was on one side of his bed; and a television easy to see and turn on with a remote rested on the nightstand.

"What would you like me to bring you tomorrow?"

"Make a few turkey sandwiches and bring some fruit. I am sure that their lunches are awful."

After that request, I was certain that he was on his way to a complete recovery. He loved to eat, and that primal instinct never left him. Furthermore, his cardiologist said that thanks to the quick intervention at Providence and the insertion of a stent within one hour after the beginning of the heart attack his heart muscle was not damaged.

I descended from the ICU to the main lobby and tried to find a taxi, hoping that some of them would be parked nearby. None was there, and after I called for one, nobody was available. I phoned our friends and neighbors asking them if they could pick me up at the hospital. I explained that my husband had had a heart attack.

"Sure, we'll be there."

I sat in the lobby for three hours before they showed up. The distance between their house and Providence was only thirty miles, their ride should not have lasted longer than half an hour. Changing their house clothes for the trip could have been done in fifteen minutes. Then I remembered how inexperienced they were regarding driving outside of their immediate neighborhood. They probably got lost despite the fact that 96 was one mile from their house and would lead them directly to the hospital. I pictured them studying the map for the longest time figuring out how to reach downtown. GPS was not yet a regular feature in cars. I got into their Toyota Celica and was overwhelmed by the reeking smell of cigarettes. They were both two-packs-a-day smokers. I told them the quickest way to my Honda and was relieved exiting theirs.

"Thank you, guys, for picking me up!"

"Keep us posted. How is he doing?!"

That night I couldn't fall asleep. My whole body ached from being tense the whole day, and my mind was processing the events of that Saturday. Thanks to some divine intervention I was home that day getting ready for my Monday trip to Italy with a group of U of M alumni. The unimaginable could have happened in my absence for which I would never have forgiven myself.

The following three days I visited my husband, bringing him sandwiches and fruit and reading the *Detroit Free Press* to him. I informed all his friends about his heart attack, and they called him, wishing him a quick recovery. Our children usually phoned in the evening to hear from me about their dad's status. He spent one week at home before the insertion of the third stent. He was sent home with a box of patches that lessened his craving for a cigarette.

"You have to stop smoking because you will not live long if you don't!"

I intentionally didn't mince my words. I wanted them to have an impact because I believed that his Kents, being overweight, and getting no exercise could really killed him. In addition, his job was stressful.

"I know. I will stop smoking," he assured me, but I had a hunch that this would be harder than he had anticipated. He had been an addict throughout his life from his college days on. He grew up in a family of cigarette smokers.

After the third stent and the used-up patches, he bought a box of Nicorette that he continues to reorder. Twelve years have passed since his heart attack, and he is still hooked on the nicotine that he chews via Nicorette the entire day. His last cigarette in our garage was not the last because nowadays when a friend offers him a cigarette, he happily accepts it and every time he goes to Meijer to pick up his medicines for the prevention of the future heart attacks, I can smell cigarette smoke on his clothes and goatee. When I point that out to him, he vehemently denies it, telling me that I am imagining it.

A few months ago, I stopped nagging because I realized the futility of it. I also think that by depriving him of an occasional cigarette, I would be adding to his stress that, according to his doctor, was the principal culprit of his heart attack. His blood pressure is under control and his cholesterol was always low. I also figured out his feelings about the idea of a last cigarette. He sees it as a metaphor for life. As long as he perceives it as the last one, and then the other last one comes along, he lives. I guess that people who once face death identify that one single thing that motivates them to get up each morning and face another day, and no one has a right to take that away from them.

FIVE

The Lake Effect

The "lake effect" is a meteorological term for describing the impact that Lake Michigan has on west Michigan winters by bringing in a large quantity of snow. I got proof of it the other day while looking through the northern exposure window of my family room. I watched white flakes ascending and accumulating on the branches of the trees and on the ground. Many limbs collapsed under the heavy snow. Throughout the day, the TV forecast issued a warning for hazardous driving conditions because the temperature below zero had caused icy conditions on roads and highways. The visibility was also diminished because of the heavy snowfall. Since I did not have to leave the house that they, I ignored the weather reports and continued admiring the fresh snow covering my yard. It was pristine, the whitest white, and shimmering when the sunrays reached it. By nightfall, the amount was over a foot high. I went to my study to check if the laser lights we had installed a week ago were able to penetrate through it. I was happy to see that they beamed their red and green colors from their posts over the snow cover, to my house facade and its roofline. The season of Christmas had begun.

The peculiar thing is that I associate the term "lake effect" with people and events that I have experienced at Lake Michigan rather than with its climatic definition. I believe that having been born under the sign of Pisces, I have a special attraction to any body of water from oceans to seas, to lakes of varied sizes, to rivers, to creeks, to ponds, even to pools. The perpetual movement of a water mass from its gentle lull to its high cresting and back to the oily calm has a therapeutic effect on my restless mind and puts me at ease with my body and myself. This is the reason I fondly remember the way Lake Michigan affected me during my family's summer visits to our friends, Robert and Kathy, who had a cottage on the lake. Built in the first half of the 20th century, the lakefront cottage resembled all the others erected high up above the sandy beach. It had three levels and a large deck facing the lake. Inside, the floor had an ugly yellow and red-checkered carpet, had dark antique furniture, and was full of different knick-knacks. The entire place smelled musty because of the humidity brought in by the lake, and it took several hours to air it out. On each bedroom and bathroom door hung directions about how to wipe sand from footwear before entering. There were also written rules about what to do before leaving the cottage. We always found everything in perfect order, and we left it neat as requested. The author of these demands and the owner of the cottage was our friend Robert's father. The man kept everything that he had ever bought, and he neatly organized his purchases in piles that he distributed throughout his other properties. He was an orderly hoarder.

One hundred wooden steps with a shaky old railing led to the beach. Before our descent, Robert would always issue his usual laconic suggestions:

"Bathroom time! Check the beach gear! Avoid climbing up!"

Once on the beach we would spread blankets on the hot sand, distribute toys to our children, one of theirs and two of ours, and sit on the low foldable chairs. We would watch the kids running along the edge of the lake, building castles in the sand, and chasing butterflies. We would take long barefoot walks looking down on our feet treading in the sand. Our chatter and laughter would spook birds hidden in the tall grass grown on the side of the beach furthest from the lake. They would fly away when they heard us coming.

In the evening, Robert would prepare his favorite summer cocktail, a Mae Tai. He would decorate it with a colorful paper umbrella and an edible orchid. While sipping it on the deck, we would talk about our different upbringing and trivial subjects, tell dirty jokes after the kids were asleep, gossip about mutual friends, and decide what we were going to do the next day. We were all relaxed and happy. Sometimes if we were not too tired or lazy, we would take the children to the beach and roast marshmallows after having dug a pit in the sand to protect the fire from the wind.

I still remember the sounds of those evenings: birds chirping through the thick foliage of the trees around the cottage, waves crashing on the shore, and Robert's wry humor when he commented on something that one of us said. He was a tall, handsome, athletic man of Dutch origin as are many other people in west Michigan. There was something noble and yet earthy about him; he was a man of his word and trustworthy. He always said what he meant, but in his held back, measured way. His greeting hugs were sincere and warm, but he could not bear the embraces that are customary for Slavic and Mediterranean people. He would put his arms around you, but his tall posture remained unbending. It was obvious that he was not used to hugging as an expression of emotions. His embrace felt unnatural, but we continued to hug each other.

One morning Robert suggested that he and my husband take a metal canoe to the lake. Our three-year old daughter wanted to go with them. She agreed to wear a safety vest but refused to let go of a slice of white bread before entering the canoe. The men swiftly paddled through the short waves away from the shore. Suddenly, I heard our daughter crying. I thought that she was either cold or scared or had some other reason for wanting to return to the beach. Robert's shout explained why she was crying:

"Her bread fell in the lake."

I was not surprised that the loss of a slice of bread caused our daughter's dismay. She was the only child that I knew who loved to eat chicken liver and kidneys that her dad would sauté for her after soaking them first in the milk. She was also able to consume an entire stick of butter without making herself sick.

I also remember one weekend at the cottage with Robert and his second wife Elisabeth, pregnant with their first child at that time. We tempered our lake routine out of consideration for her close due date. Our jokes were all on their forthcoming challenges of parenting. We arrived on Saturday morning, quickly unpacked, and rushed to the beach not wanting to waste one of the last sunny days of late August. Our children were the first to dive into the lake. We were surprised to see them splashing each other and treading water because Lake Michigan is usually too cold to stay in for more than a few minutes even in the summer. However, on that day, the sudden surge of a warm current made it swimmable. All of us stayed in the lake for hours. We played catch with the ball, swam, and chased each other. Elisabeth floated in her bright red one-piece bathing suit that accentuated her protruding belly. We could spot her from afar, which was important in case she needed help. In the evening the children were exhausted and did not need convincing to go to bed. The adults shortened their cocktail hour on the deck and headed to their bedrooms. The next morning, we got up early and rushed to the beach. Again, the children were the first to enter the lake but quickly turned around and ran back to the beach. The water had become frigid overnight, and yesterday's balmy temperature was a fluke.

Those weekends spent in a damp-smelling old cottage at Lake Michigan are unforgettable. I loved the slow-moving pace and quiet musings altered by hardy laughs at the beach, on the deck, and at mealtimes. I would let my usual guard slip into a mellow state of being. I was sad to hear that Robert's father sold his cottage to a couple who built a mansion next to it and blare loud music all day long.

Many years later, I spent one weekend at the Lake Michigan cottage of a friend of mine from work. It was early October and unusually cool. The Frank Lloyd Wright style old cottage did not have built-in heating, and we had to turn on several small electric heaters to warm up the bedrooms in the evening. The days were sunny, but the sand on the beach remained too cold to walk barefoot on it. The lake was calm and its surface gray. My friend and I took walks in the woods behind the cottage. We did not talk much, and the silence did not bother me. The forest emitted its own sounds from the crackling of branches and rustling of leaves under our feet. That stay at the lake had a different atmosphere. The gaiety was missing, words were measured, and I censored myself not to engage in controversy. I was unable to let myself just be in the moment.

My friend usually rents her cottage throughout the summer. On my recommendation, our friends Dana and Albert, decided to rent it from her for the duration of one week in August. They invited me to spend a few days with them. I came alone because my husband was working that weekend, and our children were already adults leading their own lives. After having missed an exit, I drove an additional three hours to finally reach the cottage. My tardiness put them off a bit because by waiting for my arrival, they wasted the day just sitting around. They were the type of people whose idea of a fun vacation was to engage in as many activities as possible. For example, they rode bikes, paddled in their canoe, and took long walks with their dog. It was hard for them to understand how I could spend the entire day on the beach sunbathing, doing crossword puzzles, reading magazines, and swimming when I feel like it. My definition of a relaxed vacation supports the idea of following one's moods, not having planned days, and forgetting one's routine.

Dana and Albert liked the cottage's proximity to the beach and the charcoal grill on the deck for preparing their dinners, but they complained about the household's lack of organization. They spoke of having a hard time finding linens and towels because renters would misplace them, and nobody would come afterwards to sort them out and put them in their right place. Furthermore, the overall chaotic inside of the cottage stemmed from the fact that the dwelling has been in my friend's family for generations and each generation left its stamp on it by bringing in different household items. For sentimental reasons nobody wanted to throw anything away.

The first evening Albert grilled hamburgers, we had plenty of wine, and he talked about his travels to different countries. He mentioned France, his father's yacht anchored somewhere in the Mediterranean Sea, and his skiing in the Alps. He did not brag; he just stated facts and incorporated them into a broader narrative of events that he had experienced. I liked him for his modesty and for not taking himself overly seriously. Growing up in a well-to-do Texan family, he had opportunities in life that I lacked, but listening to him talking, I never felt inferior. I also loved his deadpan humor that I always mistook for a true story, which delighted him. Dana also had a great sense of humor. Only a few people that I know can tell a joke and deliver its punchline with such gusto and delight. My weekend with the two of them was indeed great fun.

This famous "lake effect" can indeed end up affecting many levels of one's existence; on mine without a doubt, it left a lasting memory of years past.

Pride Month

The other day on my daily walk on Burton Street I spotted rainbow-colored flags hanging over the porches of two small ranch-style houses encircled by recently mowed lawns and flower beds with blue alliums and purple and white hydrangeas in full bloom. Those flags made me think of my friend Carl who passed away while driving his Cadillac into a tree at the end of a short slope next to the freeway. He died alone from a massive heart attack twelve years ago. By the time a passing car stopped and called the ambulance it was too late to jolt his heart into beating. His son called me a day later with the sad news. I was on his list of close friends. He waited for his brother's arrival in town to make the funeral arrangements together.

I informed my husband, Dave, about Carl's passing. Both of us, overwhelmed by grief, spent the day talking about him. The loss of him was hard to bear because he was an important part of our lives for more than forty years. Especially memorable were our summers together at Lake Michigan. For a month, we would rent an old cottage situated above the sandy shore and separated from the beach by one hundred wooden steps. The place was large enough to accommodate both our families, his wife, Brenda, and their two boys, and ours with our son and daughter. The rest of the year, we would celebrate the children's and the adults' birthdays together and would meet Carl and Brenda in town for a coffee and a chat.

"I don't understand how this could happen. You remember that he told us that after his first heart attack that damaged his heart muscle, his doctor prescribed several medicines to prevent any subsequent ones." My husband seemed puzzled by Carls's sudden death.

"I do remember that. He was supposed to quit smoking cigarettes, but that was challenging for him because Brenda continued to puff on two packs of Marlboros a day. The house always reeked of cigarette smoke." I tried to justify why Carl continued to light his Ronhills.

"He had elevated blood pressure for years, but I thought that he took care of it. He was never overweight and was always active, even after his retirement. His death doesn't make any sense to me," Dave, unable to accept our friend's death, continued to analyze all the factors related to Carl's health.

I stopped commenting on my husband's rationalization of Carl's passing because my thoughts flew to his and Brenda's wedding. Their reception after the civil ceremony was an intimate affair with only family members and close friends in attendance. It took place in the backyard of Brenda's father's house. Several rustic-looking tables covered with red and white checkered tablecloths were brimming with grilled meats and homemade desserts that Brenda's and Carl's mothers baked. It was a happy celebration, simple, unpretentious, perfectly suitable for Carl's nature. His famous laughter resonated in the balmy summer air.

Two years later we rented the cottage for the first time. The image of Carl and Brenda slowly descending those hundred steps is permanently etched into my brain. I watched in awe from the beach. Carl's Bermuda jean shorts accentuated his long legs, a white T-shirt clung to his lean torso, and his head full of fine, light brown, wavy hair covered half of his ears and neck. He liked to wear his hair longer even as he aged, and his locks became gray. Being 6'4" tall, he towered over Brenda's 5'8" statuesque, model-like frame. She wore an off-white linen dress, brown flip-flops, and carried a large beach bag with colorful towels spilling out over the edges. Her straight, shiny, jet-black hair reached her shoulders and was moving in the wind coming from the lake. The two of them looked like a picture-perfect couple. Each was beautiful in their own way. There was something regal in their coming down, and I wish I had taken a photo of them, but I was busy entertaining children and helping Dave blow up their vinyl tubes and swimming arm bands.

As soon as Carl stepped onto the beach, he began setting up the area where we were going to spend the day. He first spread out the picnic blanket that I brought from home, opened and dug into the sand blue and yellow stripped beach umbrella that we found in the cottage storage room, and placed a large cooler full of sandwiches, fruit, a gallon of water, and a six-packs of Founder's All Day IPA underneath it. Along the way he jokingly complained about those hundred steps.

"I hope that nobody needs to go to the bathroom."

While he was arranging our small beach camp, Brenda stood aside waiting for him to open a comfortable tall beach chair that they brought from their house. The rest of us used old, sun-bleached chairs whose seats rested on the sand. They were comfortable enough to sit on, but getting up took some effort. When Brenda saw that her chair was ready, she took off her dress and plummeted into it in her Esther Williams-style black and white, expensive-looking one-piece bathing suit. From that point on, she got up from her "throne" only twice; first to dunk her toes in the lake to assess its temperature, and second to take a five-minute stroll along the edge of the water. Carl remained in charge of our day on the beach: at noon, he distributed sandwiches, took the kids exploring in the tall grass that grew out of the sand further from the lake, and led them into the water for a brief plunge because the lake was too cold for a swim. He also made sure that the adults had a can of beer in hand. Brenda seldom spoke and only when asked a specific question. The rest of the time she would read a book, oblivious to activities taking place around her. We stayed on the beach until five o'clock because it was time to prepare dinner. The children became restless, my husband was hungry, and Brenda finished her reading.

"Guys, it's time to climb those hundred steps. Let's go!" Carl's voice was as cheerful as in the morning.

While others were taking showers, Carl and I were in the kitchen, sipping a cold chardonnay, chopping onions, garlic, and fresh tomatoes for the Bolognese sauce. He poked fun at my sun accentuated face freckles, told me dirty jokes, and we both laughed holding our stomachs and crying unable to stop. A few times after dinner, Brenda washed the dishes because the cottage didn't have a dishwasher, but Carl was the one who did it when the rest of us vacated the kitchen as soon as the dinner was over, telling him that we had to help the kids get ready for bed. Once the lights in the children's bedrooms were turned off and we couldn't hear their giggles coming through the half-closed windows any longer, the four of us would sit on the deck looking at the moon mirrored on the lake's surface and listen to the waves breaking at its edge. Brenda and I drank chardonnay, while the men enjoyed cognac. We chatted about our jobs, children, and gossiped about mutual friends. Carl interjected his lighthearted comments into each topic of conversation, thus making even the serious arguments funny. His glee could have come across as flakiness to those that didn't know him well, but that assumption could not be further from the truth. Carl was a complex man, intuitive, intelligent, a great character reader, and yet I sometimes wondered if his excessive happiness and need to please was a cover-up for some deep emotional struggle that he could not share with anyone.

Our subsequent summers at Lake Michigan were nuanced replicas of that first day on the beach. The children grew up and once they became teenagers, they grudgingly agreed to spend one month away from their friends. They entertained themselves by playing games rather than paddling with their fathers in the old metal canoe stored in the back of the cottage. As young adults they pursued their own plans for how to spend their vacations. Being empty nesters didn't bother us, and we looked forward to renting the same old cottage. Instead of spending a day on the beach, we preferred sitting on the deck talking, reading, and playing cards. In the evening, after having finished a bottle of bubbly that replaced chardonnay and cognac, we would howl at the silver moon.

I also remembered Carl's small studio above the bicycle repair shop where he and Brenda lived after they got married. He worked as a graphic designer for a local marketing firm and Brenda, who graduated with a degree in economics, found a job in a consulting agency. Despite his steady promotions at work, he couldn't shed the chip on his shoulder for never finishing college and felt inferior to Brenda. She, on the other hand, was not bothered by his lack of higher education because she genuinely loved him. Having a failed first marriage behind her, she found in Carl a soulmate and a partner who also turned out to be a great father to her son from the first marriage and their son.

They realized that living in that cramped studio space was no longer feasible and with Brenda's father's financial help they bought a colonial style house in an old neighborhood that came with a large yard, a wild cherry and a crabapple tree, overgrown boxwood bushes, and on one side a bare patch of land that the previous owners used for growing vegetables and herbs. The house needed substantial fixing, starting with the installation of a new roof, and replacing the rotted wooden railing on the long second-floor balcony. For those projects Carl hired a construction company while he took care of the yard by trimming trees and shrubs. He also mowed the lawn. Brenda planted tomatoes, cucumbers, green peppers, parsley, and basil in the bare spot by the house. She asked Carl to water her garden while he was dousing the grass because the house didn't have an automatic sprinkler system.

The interior of their new dwelling also required work. The walls needed fresh paint, and all the faucets dripped. Carl managed those jobs by himself. He also furnished the rooms with the second-hand furniture brought from his studio that he gradually replaced with new pieces. The house evolved into a home, thanks to his superb sense of aesthetics. He hung old inherited oil paintings on the newly painted antique-white walls and embellished the large living room windows with gold-colored heavy velvet puddled drapes. I always thought of their house as being Carl's because Brenda refused to be involved in any decision making.

Since they both worked full-time, Carl found a housekeeper for the daily cleaning, grocery shopping, laundry, and ironing because he thought that they should relax and spend time with their boys instead of doing chores on the weekends. Their combined income allowed them to travel, and he organized trips to Europe. They would leave the kids with Brenda's mother. His favorite destination was France, where he lived a couple of years, but they also visited Spain, Portugal, Italy, England, Ireland, Vienna, and Prague. They would stay in four-star hotels, eat in known restaurants, and do a lot of shopping. Carl would buy brand name expensive perfumes and accessories for Brenda, and for himself Cuban cigars and fashionable sunglasses.

"I wonder how they can afford those trips?"

My husband would sometimes comment after having listened to Carls's description of their abroad experiences and purchases. I asked myself the same question. Their luxury lifestyle did not apply only to their domestic and overseas trips, they also lived large throughout the year. Neither Brenda nor Carl came from money. I knew that her family lived modestly on her father's salary who, by the way, was a miser incarnate. However, she quickly got accustomed to the new way of handling money. She was buying expensive clothes and footwear, and paying for regular grooming in hair, facial, and pedicure salons. Carl enjoyed helping her choose her work and leisure wardrobe and took pride in her newly acquired polished appearance. I found that very strange because my husband never interfered in my clothing choices. If he liked what I bought he would simply say, "This looks good on you."

I had a feeling that Carl wanted Brenda to adopt his fashion sense and become a subject of admiration. While staying in Paris, his natural instincts for beauty sharpened. He visited museums filled with classical and modern art, learned about the architecture, and observed the way French women and men dressed. Following their example, he preferred to buy a few high-quality clothing items and pointed those out to Brenda. However, he willingly skipped purchasing a new seasonal wardrobe for himself if the boys wanted popular toys, signed up for different sports, or insisted on having clothes that their teenage friends wore. He also paid their college tuition. Brenda remained oblivious to their financial status as long as her wishes came through and she was free of any accountability. Carl never told her about having to borrow money to pay the regular monthly bills and maxing out his credit cards. His life turned into a juggling act of taking bank loans, relying on friends' generosity, and at the end he owed a hefty sum of money to loan sharks tied to organized crime.

As years passed, we noticed the first cracks developing in their seemingly perfect union. Their public bickering became more frequent, and several of our mutual friends began to avoid their company. We witnessed the same unpleasant exchanges of bitter, often sarcastic verbal exchanges during our Michigan Lake vacations. His once upbeat behavior toned down. What struck us as particularly odd was that a couple of times Carl would interrupt his stay in the cottage saying that his team at work urgently needed him because they encountered a problem while working on a new project. He would leave and return after two days in a completely different mood. He was again his jovial self, cracking jokes, and being tolerant of Brenda's frequent outbursts of anger. The same pattern of both planned and sudden business-related trips continued when we got back to the city. Brenda never questioned him while they always happened during weekends.

"Where the hell does he go? Who has business dealings over the weekend?" my husband asked me one day.

"Perhaps he rents a hotel or motel room somewhere to get away from Brenda and relax," I guessed.

When Carl confided to him that Brenda had become difficult to live with not only because of her unstoppable appetite for spending, permanent moodiness, and a taste for multiple glasses of Riesling each day, his short escapades sounded like a reasonable solution for saving their marriage. He also began to see a therapist, another positive sign. One day I was sipping my macchiato at Starbucks, when one of our friends saw me and brought her cappuccino over to join me. After a short briefing about our lives, she leaned over the table and whispered:

"Yesterday afternoon John saw Carl entering Exile bar in the company of a young man."

"So what? He probably took a coworker for a drink."

"It's a gay bar! Why didn't he take him to any other bar?"

She insisted that I express my take on that revelation of hers, but I decided to shut off her innuendo:

"What do you want me to say? We should not jump to conclusions. Perhaps Exile makes good cocktails."

We were in the late '80s, in a decade that preceded Matthew Shepard's murder in 1998 which opened a discussion about the gay community in America and the country's stand on human rights violated by on-the-rise hate crimes. It took eleven years to enact the Matthew Shepard Hate Crimes Prevention Act in 2009. A portion of the baby boomer generation had a tough time recognizing and accepting those that were different from them, forcing gay man and women to hide and live lives of compromise.

When I connected the dots of Carls's behavior over the years, it became clear to me that he belonged to that group of shadow members of society. I recall him telling us about two burglaries in his house when they were vacationing. Only one of the thieves was arrested and charged; the other was never caught. The police report stated that both break-ins indicated an unforced entry. Moreover, none of the rooms were ransacked, a clear sign that the burglars knew where the valuables were. I concluded that Carl must have invited each man to the house when Brenda and the boys were vacationing. They must have been his lovers that he picked up at different gay bars in town.

Carl began to avoid all intimacy with Brenda using excuses such as being tired, stressed, and having migraine headaches. Brenda bought into his lies and compensated her need for affection by having multiple affairs with married men. Since I heard about them through the grapevine, I never dared to ask her about it despite our long friendship. I wondered if she even considered the possibility that Carl might have been gay. The following question of hers revealed that such a conclusion never crossed her mind. She wanted to know my opinion about her recent gathering with Carl's friends.

"Do you know who was there? Three gay guys and two lesbians, one of them pregnant. I don't know how Carl knows these people. What do you think?"

I paused for a second, feeling cornered and deciding on my answer. I had a fleeting thought that the party was organized for Brenda to indirectly reveal to her Carl's true identity but looking at the genuinely puzzled expression on her face, I realized that she would brush off the truth because it would defy her Catholic upbringing. A denial offered an easy way out of her moral conundrum.

"Carl knows a lot of people through his work and being always friendly he is welcomed in any company."

I lied because I knew that my revelation would not set her free. It would force her to make a life altering decision, and she was not ready for it. She needed Carl for all practical aspects of her life because she was either unable or not willing to give up her comforts and override her self-centeredness for a greater good—his freedom. For a long time, I felt guilty for not truthfully answering Brenda's question.

They remained married, she in her world and he in his, in which in time a reciprocal compromise evolved into a feeling of mutual sacrifice. Carl didn't want to leave his family because he loved being a father and grandfather, taking care not only of Brenda and their sons but also of his extended family and friends in need. I think that he regretted depriving Brenda of the husband she deserved to have, and to compensate for that he placed her at the center of their illusionary perfect marriage. He continued to be devoted to her even when her early dementia affected her ability to function independently. He would give her simple house chores to do during the day to engage her brain. She watered potted plants and emptied the dishwasher, to mention the main ones. After his retirement and their sons pursuing their careers elsewhere, Carl became the willing principal caregiver to Brenda. He could have placed her in a facility for people in her condition but that would have been contrary to his character as an exemplary human being, loyal, compassionate, and loving.

With Pride Month on its way, the rainbow flags flying in the wind, and people around the globe marching for LGBTQ communities' inclusion into all social structures, I ask myself a rhetorical question if Carl would have joined their walk. He would not have because he safeguarded his privacy and his family's. The unforgiving '80s were deep-seated in his psyche. Instead, he would be sitting in his recliner, smoking a cigar, and contentedly watching the parade on the TV. Carl remained hidden in his closet, aware that it was not his time to come out. The price for living on his terms would have been too high because the larger society was not ready for him. He sealed his identity to comply with social norms that held keys to his self-determination. I, on the other hand, accepted him with no reservations because he was bigger than life and yet the most tragic man I have ever known. To honor him, I will march today holding high the rainbow flag with his name written on it.

SIX

The Pumpkin Field

The freeway that takes Ana to work and back is one of those boring roads that curves only three to four times in a stretch of thirty miles. On its left and right side there are mostly cornfields alternated with a few wooded hills. While driving she notices when seasons change, but that does not affect her mood. The monotony of the landscape paired with her daily routine drive dulled her senses over the years.

Unexpectedly, one afternoon on Ana's return from work, an unusual scene caught her eye. On her right - just before a bridge overpass, that she had passed hundreds of times - she saw a large field full of pumpkins spread across it. They varied in size and were bright orange with green vines at the top. They looked as if someone had placed them there by design the night before.

"This is unreal. I didn't notice them growing," Ana thought.

She spotted a man standing by his car on the shoulder of the freeway taking pictures. The entire sight of a man who stopped to photograph those pumpkins made Ana happy and feeling alive. She felt an instant alliance with this stranger. At that moment, she wanted to be in his photo sitting in the middle of that field of pumpkins.

"Perhaps we drive the same road every day following or passing each other? And here we are, finally meeting, even for just a few seconds, amused by the rupture in our routine," Ana concluded.

She did not stop her car to enter the man's picture because it was just a fleeting moment of delight, like many others that she safeguarded in her memory and recalled with nostalgia. She knew that the pumpkins would be harvested before Halloween and carved into grotesque faces lit inside with a candle. They would stand on the front porch to greet trick-or-treaters. A few days later and half rotten, they usually end up in the trash. This analogy dimmed her desire to partake in the man's photo because she did not want to become a part of the pumpkins' fleeting beauty.

"I don't want to become a pumpkin and simply dissolve," she thought, completing the last turn before reaching her house.

This state of Ana's mind not to accept things transitory or permanent for what they are was due to her deep-seated unhappiness with her life. The predictable monotony of each day depleted her energy to change the course of her existence. Her mood fluctuated from boredom to emptiness. Her sense of leading an unfulfilling life was overwhelming. She realized that self-pity was not a solution nor were accusations darted at those close to her. She could not single out a source that caused this imbalance in her well-being. To the outside world, she was a success story – a solid marriage, bright children, and an interesting job.

"I don't know what is happening to me; it's totally alien to my nature. I used to be a doer, found solutions," Ana tried to rationalize her feelings.

"I feel like I am being dragged through each day. I wake up every morning at six-thirty, more tired than before I went to bed. The ringing of the alarm clock is enough to make me hate the whole world and myself boarding in it. I go through the next hour and a half semi-consciously, talking to myself in order not to forget anything that I should do before leaving the house: the children's lunches are ready, their waffles are in the toaster, and my daughter's glasses are in her book bag. My coffee is always cold because I forgot to drink it."

"Paul, wake up. It's seven-fifteen," I call out to our son.

I should change this sentence once in a while. Maybe the word order:

"It is seven-fifteen. Wake up, Paul!" or "It is seven, Paul, and fifteen. Wake up!" or "Fifteen past seven. Up wake, Paul!"

"I cannot alter the semantics of the sentence, but at least I can try to modify the tone of my voice that has remained the same throughout the years. I sound like a voice from a hotel wake up call. Psychologists say that children need a routine because it gives them the necessary sense of security and stability. Paul certainly gets an adult dose of it every morning, and it should last him a lifetime."

"Honey, school time! Mama will carry you to the family room and give you breakfast. Here are your clothes."

"I repeat the same sentence to our daughter, Lana, every morning, lacking other expressions to make her morning more cheerful. I don't want to change this sequence of my daughter's morning routine. She is younger than her brother, and she needs more words. Words matter; they always do. At her age they should be comforting, reassuring, cuddling, and motherly."

At five to eight, Ana and her children are ready for departure. Her attire is business-like, a gray suit with a dark red buttoned up silk blouse. The children sit in the back of the car being noisy, happy, and looking forward to seeing their school friends. Ana likes to see them this way, owning their day from the start. She remembered her childhood in the former Yugoslavia being very different. When she was seven and began grade school, both her parents worked. They left for work at six thirty and set up the alarm clock to wake her up at seven. They would place the alarm clock on a metal plate to resonate twice as loud, just to make sure that she heard it. She would skip her breakfast, get dressed in a hurry, and lock the apartment door before heading to school. She walked a mile, crossed several busy streets, and met her friends along the way.

Her first meal of the day was a snack provided by the school thanks to the UNRRA rations that helped feed Europe after the Second World War. It consisted of a small bottle of the powder-made chocolate milk and a cold bun with a slice of the American cheese. The cheese would stick to Ana's palate, and she had a hard time swallowing it. Once in high school, she and the other students would bring their own snacks because the UNRRA stopped providing them. She was happy not to eat American cheese any longer. The school day would end at one o' clock in the afternoon, and she would return to an empty apartment. She waited for her parents' arrival at three when her mother would prepare a combined lunch/dinner meal. At times Ana had to put potatoes to boil while doing her homework. Thinking about her childhood, she regretted that it was too short.

Ana's husband, Mark, does not get up before the house sounds vacant. He drinks his coffee hot while shaving. His morning routine is unobstructed by the bustle of children or Ana's rushed steps from the shower to the kitchen, to the children's rooms, back to the kitchen, opening and closing the refrigerator, and turning on the toaster.

"Lucky fellow! I would love to drink my coffee while hot – even warm – and read the newspaper without constantly checking the clock," Ana often wished.

Mark never offered any help in the morning, neither with getting the children ready for school nor with driving them to the bus stop or one of them to school. On those days when her schedule was crammed with job-related tasks and the children's need to drive them to their after-school activities, she would seek his help to pick up Paul, whose tennis lessons were far from their house. In the meantime, she would cook dinner and pick up Lana from the ballet studio located just down the road. It would also have been helpful if Mark had dropped Paul off at his school in the morning. He passed by it on his way to work. This would require him to get up half an hour earlier than he wanted. Ana drove eight miles in the opposite direction from the freeway that she took going to her job in order to get Paul to his school. This added sixteen more miles to her daily thirty.

They had many discussions in which she tried to explain to Mark about being overwhelmed with house chores, caring for the entire family, and her job. Demands on her seemed to increase at a rapid pace. Throughout her plea for some help, he usually stared at the TV, half listening, half tuned out. He would justify his non-involvement by having a stressful job that consumed him. At this point, desperate that he did not meet her demands even in a small measure, Ana would raise her voice to get his full attention. Mark would get angry because she failed to acknowledge his financial contribution to the family's standard of living. They never reconciled their different positions, and each of those initially calm discussions would escalate into huge, hurtful fights.

Gradually Ana gave up trying to solicit any help from Mark. It became a weary task, and she was too tired to pursue it. She continued doing everything by herself. The children and the house were hers to manage.

Once she dropped Paul off at school and Lana at the bus station, Ana's professional job began. After three hours of classroom teaching, two office hours, several more cups of coffee, and no time for lunch, she was exhausted. Her brain was multitasking even when she was supposed to focus only on her lecture. Sometimes in the middle of a sentence, questions would flash through her mind:

"Did I take the meat out of the freezer?"

"Does Paul have his house key? Did I tell him to keep an eye on his sister?"

Ana wished that at least while she worked, she would be able to disconnect the part of her brain that always gravitated to motherhood. She never succeeded. Her social interaction at work was limited to a few exchanged words with colleagues and friends in the hallways. Nobody said anything meaningful, and quite often did not even hear each other's questions nor listen to the answers.

"How are you?"

"Fine, "Ana would utter her noncommittal answer.

"Which classes are you teaching?"

"Do you always teach in the basement? I personally hate it. And you?"

She was often tempted to say but never did because it would be rude: "Yes, I hate the basement. I hate correcting tests, I hate textbooks, and most of all I despise our damn civilized American coolness about everything. Does anybody ever have a headache, gas pains, a sick child, a boring week? We all try so hard to reveal only that personal information that does not tarnish our standing and image among the people we work with. We do not want to be judged or become the subject of a title-tattle. Spontaneity somehow became synonymous with not being proper. Why do we all measure our words like they are worth gold?"

Ana's mother taught her from an early age how to behave and talk properly. She insisted on good manners: greet people on arrival and departure, do not to talk and laugh too loudly, listen more and talk less especially about oneself, eat with your mouth closed and cover it with your hand when yawning, close the door gently instead of slamming it, and the list goes on. She would correct her whenever her behavior was contrary to her teachings. Ana never completely regained that child spontaneity, but living far from her mother enabled her to develop a sense of humor, and she allowed herself to laugh as loudly as it pleased her. At work, she followed the protocol of the admissible behavioral code to the letter. She thought if she strayed from it, her colleagues would brand her ill-mannered and politically incorrect, characteristics unacceptable at an institution of higher learning. She smiled a lot, and talked little, and this shielded her from being a topic of the department's gossip.

At two o'clock in the afternoon, Ana was behind the wheel rushing home in time for her children's afternoon snack and driving Paul to his tennis practice and Lana to her ballet class. The forty-five-minute wait for Lana's class to end tested her level of tolerance for the other mothers' chitchat. Sitting idle on a chair reserved for the waiting parents, she could not avoid hearing the other mothers' vapid conversations. She would prefer to correct students' tests or just read the newspaper, something that she did not have time to do in the morning. The voices around her were loud, breaking her concentration needed for any meaningful task.

"Did you buy Jenny a Cabbage Patch?" a high-pitched question pierced the air.

"No, they're too expensive here, but if you go to Windsor, Canada, with the dollar being so strong, it's really a bargain," a nasal voice answered.

"I'm 736th on the Toys R Us waiting list for a Cabbage Patch. I hope I get it by Christmas."

"Did you know that Debby had her baby last week after Lora's class? Her sister-in-law is also expecting any day. If I were in her shoes, I would stop coming here. Her husband can drive the kid," the nasal voice changed the subject.

Ana could barely stand listening to the mothers talk. During those long forty-five minutes, every other woman in the room was just about to deliver; the others half expressed their desire to be pregnant, and they all adored motherhood and crocheting. They were McDonald's mothers, PTA mothers, soccer mothers, but Ana called them by the generic title MOTHERS in capital letters. By comparing herself to MOTHERS, Ana felt inferior.

"Am I a bad mother? I drive my children only 200 miles weekly. Every day I serve dinner at seven, made all from scratch and nutritionally well-balanced despite complaints by one or more of my family members that refuse to eat that day's vegetable or meat. Their whining annoys me, but not to the point that I give up on preparing healthy dinners. I feel unappreciated because after two hours spent cooking, hand washing large pots, and placing the other dishes in the dishwasher, nobody says "thank you." I expect Mark to lead by example and teach our children how to express their gratitude when I or somebody else does something nice for them. After dinner there are other chores that I need to finish: put one load of laundry in the washer, check the children's homework, and occasionally help them with it, and by that time my personality is extinguished."

Listening and observing those MOTHERS, Ana realized where her sense of inferiority by comparison with them came from. She had a full-time job and most of them were homemakers. They had time to enjoy every phase of their children's growth, which made them happy. Their lives did not spread in a zillion directions as did hers. She felt guilty not having a leisure breakfast with her children, greeting them at the bus stop when they returned from school, playing games after dinner, and riding bikes with them. She considered herself an adequate mother, and she knew that by covering all their essential needs she was actually masking her guilt for not being just theirs.

At eleven o clock in the night, Ana was sitting exhausted and semi-conscious on the sofa, trying to stay awake. The TV was on, but the images she saw through her half-closed eyes were blurred.

"How was your day?" This was Mark's usual question.

"Nothing special. The usual stuff. I talked to Freda and Zeta. They are O.K. How about yours?"

Ana decided not to tell him about the pumpkins she saw that day because he would not understand the happiness that brought her. He was not a nature enthusiast; thus, he did not pay much attention to the diverse landscapes that they encountered while traveling both in the country and abroad.

"The usual stuff, you know," was her husband's habitual, laconic reply because he did not want to miss the 11:00 pm news.

Ana didn't know how his day was or any other day he spent at work. He seldom talked about it because he lacked the content for a trivial narrative. She knew that he did not register events and people around him because they did not interest him. His profession was his cocoon that shielded him from the outside world. At times if there was something that bothered him, he would open up and share his feelings. Ana always listened carefully but restrained her comments because he was easily irritated, especially if she was right by pointing out how he could have handled the situation better. Their marriage suffered because of this scarcity of sharing experiences and feelings. It seemed as if both safeguarded the core of their being for their personal reasons –Ana for not wanting to be rejected and for avoiding any conflict, and Mark for not feeling the need to deal with his and her emotions.

By midnight Ana was finally in bed, but not yet asleep. Mark walked into their bedroom and lay in bed next to her. They made love quite often. It was the final segment of their day. They approached it as athletes who walk into a gym with a goal in mind. All the equipment was there. They knew how to use it to achieve the expected result. Eros somehow got lost in the clinical motion of their bodies.

"Something is missing in our love making. It is probably me. I am seldom motivated because I am exhausted. I have lost my sense of self. Our late-night lovemaking has become a routine, one last thing to do at the end of a long day. I might feel differently if there were a bit of a romantic decorum," Ana concluded.

They finished making love. Claire set the alarm clock for six-thirty. It was half an hour past midnight. She pulled the covers to her chin and stared at the ceiling.

"I think that I have dissolved into one giant orange pumpkin," Ana thought as her body became heavy, and her closed eyelids chased away night shadows.

The Squid and the Whale

It was one of those lazy January winters that Michiganders called mild because the temperatures did not dip below zero, and the snow did not reach the top of their boots. They continued to wear their puffer coats because the weather could quickly turn for the worse, and a blue sky could suddenly become gray and heavy with snow erasing its promise of letting the sun's rays deliver warmth. While picking up the *Detroit Free Press* from the mailbox one Monday morning, I decided to spend the afternoon at the movies. I wanted to see *The Squid and the Whale*, and invited a friend of mine, Claudia, to join me. We bought the senior citizen matinee tickets and two large plastic glasses of a cheap chardonnay from the concession stand. The young woman handed us the mandatory bright green bracelets along with our wine. We sat in the middle of the last row of balcony seats to be as far as possible from the screen and the loud soundtrack. I had trouble inserting a straw in my glass, and Claudia helped me by poking her finger through the small hole in its cover. I saw that gesture of hers as being more than a solution to a simple problem; it comforted me at the time I needed it. I knew that I could count on her whenever I felt helpless and lost in my solitude.

The movie began. Its theme was the break-up of a marriage and the impact it had on the children. Not understanding the extent of their parents' unhappiness, they suffered watching them argue. At the same time, the children tried to define their own place in the new relationships their parents forged. I liked the movie. The dialogues were well written and acted, the director and the cinematographer did a fine job, but more important than the artistic merits of the film was its principal topic that made me think about my own marriage in relation to my existence.

"What is my reality? Why do I suddenly feel an urgency to face it or explain it?" I asked myself while driving back home. I guess, eventually, everyone introspects his or her own life, trying to identify what makes it both unique and ordinary at the same time. I am sure that many people walked in my shoes, and others would follow after me as well. At fifty-seven years old, soon to be fifty-eight, I finally feel ready to claim ownership of all things that I've done in my life, good and bad, and forgive myself for wrongs I have inflicted and exculpate those that have hurt me. I have reached clarity in my thinking, the courage to face controversies, and I no longer fear those who might judge me or reject me. This sense of self-worth stems from my realization that I do not owe anything to anybody, nor do I expect any reciprocity for my good deeds.

Contemplating my marriage, I have to admit that it did improve, thanks to a reversal of my take on it. I no longer view a compromise in our relationship as a synonym for perpetual frustration. For example, I hate my husband's chain-smoking two packs of Kent in our family room daily because my clothes smell and my hair reeks as if I have spent an evening in the Moose Saloon. All my efforts in convincing him to quit have failed. The health hazard from second-hand smoke is a scientific fact, but he still doubts its veracity. I do not know any children exposed to so much cigarette smoke as did ours while growing up. Thankfully, they did not follow their father's example, and now they are both devoted non-smokers.

"I am going to watch TV in the basement," I calmly informed my husband one evening, not wanting to inhale the polluted air any longer.

"Ok," he answered without looking at me. Comfortably stretched on our long sectional, he proceeded to watch science fiction programs on the TV and the computer screen in front of him simultaneously. His ashtray was filling up fast with half-smoked cigarettes. He was in his comfort zone, and did not care to find out why I decided not to spend the evening with him in the same room. I took one last look at him before heading downstairs and thought about our thirty-three years together without having a deep connection that usually accompanies long unions. I was only twenty-four years old when we got married. I wondered if I really knew what I wanted or expected from a marriage.

My decision to wed was neither emotional nor rational. I complied with the social norm subscribed for college-educated women of my generation to marry soon after graduation. We followed each other in pursuing the fulfillment of our professional ambitions and exploring our sexuality within a legally binding union called marriage. Some of us thought of marriage as a path to the personal freedom that our authoritarian parents suppressed throughout our growing up. They believed to have the birthright to control all aspects of their daughters' lives as long as they lived.

My image of a marriage was a blueprint of my parents'. I understood it as a partnership between two people who endure and weather challenging times together and tolerate each other's shortcomings. The word "love" was not in their vocabulary, and I seldom witnessed tenderness between them. They frequently argued about money and household chores but were on the same page regarding major purchases for the family such as buying their first car, a blue Ford Pinto, and deciding where to go on vacation. My mother would initiate all their fights because she always was mad about something. My father would withdraw from those heated verbal conflicts most of the time, and he stayed an hour longer in the office the next day. At times, being angry at each other they would not talk for several days. I hated that silence. Despite their character differences, they never considered a divorce and remained married until their death when they were in their nineties.

From my parents' home I entered the institution of marriage unaware of who I was and what I wanted in life overall. I am sure that my husband was equally a blank page as I was because our parents did most of the thinking and decision making for us up to the day of our wedding. We both were clueless about how we were going to define our future life together. It took us years to learn about our own selves first and then about each other, which brings me to today's metaphorical question: "Am I the squid or the whale in our marriage?"

I harbor traits of both sea creatures. I am able to extend in many directions and in that, I mimic the squid's tentacles, which have far-reaching control and restrict impulses coming from its head. I define my tentacles as emotions that often follow an unpredicted path. At times, they are volatile but turn quickly steady when somebody needs my help. I also extend my tentacles toward different passions of mine. For example, in grade school I showed an interest in acting and performed in school plays that lasted until I graduated from high school. I even wanted to study acting at the Theater Academy, but my mother convinced me that being an actor is a risky profession that would not guarantee job security. She insisted that I study foreign languages because she thought that such a degree would land me a job on television as a broadcaster. Her dream of me being a TV personality clashed with my idea of a career I wanted to pursue. Being the mother of a known person would enable her to brag to her girlfriends that she was instrumental in my professional success. I did end up studying foreign languages and comparative literature, which opened the door into great literary works that I read in the original tongue. Instead of working as a translator, I chose to teach.

Writing remains another passion of mine, as is reading, interior design, and traveling. My widespread tentacles give me the freedom to explore the vast unknown and to circumvent rules and morals that could stop me doing it. However, as the squid's head controls the tentacles' movements, mine keeps my actions in check since the birth of my two children. They taught me how to grow up and become a responsible adult. I see them as a cosmic gift bestowed upon me to protect me until the end of my time. I would never let my tentacles detach from my head because that would unbalance them and pull the rug out from under their sense of security, thus harming them in more than one way.

Despite my carefully crafted equilibrium between my desires and my rational mind, there is always in me that little mermaid from the bottom of the ocean that strives to resurface and reshape her life into an unbound existence. I know that I would never fully reemerge, but I am also sure of not remaining on the seabed. My tentacles pull me up to join other squids and swim along in our shared ocean of uncertainty, doubts, and compromises.

My whale persona forbids me to accept any defeat. I believe that my mind can reign over any matter that befalls me. For example, I have a high tolerance for pain both physical and emotional, and I maintain full control of it in situations in which others would fold. I have taught myself to be strong and fearlessly defend what is dear and essential to my well-being. However, I sometimes lose and have to accept my defeat, but prior to having explored all options, I do not concede to not achieving a favorable outcome for a problem I am facing. Any loss does not paralyze my movements forward. I continue to swim toward other opportunities just like a whale that cruises from warmer waters to cold ones in search of food. What sustains me when the odds are against me is my credo that everything bad eventually will end.

Being a squid and a whale has had both a positive and a negative impact on my marriage. Several characteristics of both animals I brought with me; the others I gradually developed. If I had not rushed into wifehood, I would have been able to modify them, making bad ones less pronounced and accentuating good ones. I blindly entered my marriage in both a literal and symbolic sense. My husband was the blind date that a friend of mine arranged because he was the best friend of her boyfriend and did not have a girlfriend. Moreover, she thought that I needed to meet somebody new after I had walked away from the years-long, bruising relationship that drowned in its own drama without a resolution. I thought that he was handsome and manly looking. He seemed comfortable in his skin and was easy to talk to. He also exuded an aura of melancholy that led to his taciturnity years later. He was a man without a torrid past and the baggage that my former boyfriend carried. After having dated several months, I liked him enough to marry him. I believed to have landed in a promising relationship that would develop into a true partnership and an emotionally satisfying union. Unfortunately, our marriage never moved beyond being promising.

We sailed through our graduate schools, had our first child, a boy, and the second one, a girl. My husband eventually cocooned in his own world. It consisted of his work that he often despised, his favorite TV programs, Schwarzenegger's action movies, his computer, and the bestsellers that he read. The rest of us existed like theater props and the background noise on a stage that he created. I was a teacher, a cook, a housekeeper, our children's driver, and an occasional collocutor when there was nothing interesting on television. When I took turns talking, my sentences had to be short and focused on points that I tried to make. A longer narrative bored him because it would infringe on his preplanned flow of the evening hours. Where married life failed me, my work became a source of great satisfaction because my students valued my teaching competence, and I felt to matter. Seeing my children growing up well-adjusted and happy filled me with pride and joy. They never caused me any grief as if they knew that I could not bear any other disappointment. A disconnected marriage was enough.

Our children are adults now and live on their own. They love their partners who love them in return. Who am I now? Am I a squid or a whale? I still think that I am both. I no longer expect my husband to pull me up from the ocean's floor to its surface. I did it all by myself. I float stretched on my back, feeling the gentle breeze caressing my body and the tiny waves washing over me. I imagine the whales' giant fins moving up and down while their bodies spiral and the squids releasing the ink over their tentacles. I am in perfect unison with nature and finally letting my guard down because there is nobody that can pull me down.

The Wedding

Nora slouched on the grey leather couch opposite her husband Doug, who stretched out on an identical sofa fast asleep. It was two o'clock, the time for his usual nap after lunch. His head rested on the already flattened, once puffy decorative pillows, and the white cotton blanket under him needed washing, Nora concluded. She watched his placid face covered with a three-day stubble, his grey hair a bit messy, and the TV remote clutched in his hand as if he was afraid that she would yank it from him and select the program that she preferred to see instead of watching the science fiction movies that he liked. She listened to his rhythmic breathing with his mouth slightly ajar. It was a familiar scene that made her cognizant of the fact that they had both settled into a state of total acceptance and reached a level of comfort that most couples experience after being married for fifty years. All the turbulence and hardship related to their careers, to raising children, and to moving to different cities were behind them. The only occasional worry that Nora and Doug had was their health, especially his. She thought about their upcoming fiftieth anniversary at the end of October and remembered Doug's take on it.

"What do you want to do?"

"I don't know. What do you propose we do?"

"You decide. I am okay with anything you want."

"Usually, kids organize something for their parents' celebration. At least this is what I have heard from other people."

"Ours are not going to do anything. They are too busy with their own lives."

"You are right. Let's go to the movies. We haven't gone since the beginning of the Covid pandemic."

"There is nothing new playing that I am eager to see. I don't care about films based on superheroes. They are really boring and one-dimensional."

"Okay. I don't like them either. Why don't I make us a nice dinner, and we'll watch something on Netflix?"

"Perfect. Let's do that, and we could take a trip to the Caribbean in February."

"Agreed."

This conversation was typical of their retirement years. They liked to keep things low-key and mutually accommodating. Nora often wondered how their marriage had endured after a rocky start. By today's standards they were both young when they got married - she was twenty-four and Doug was twenty-six years old. If not for her unplanned pregnancy, they probably would have split because they had opposite temperaments: she was outgoing, easy to talk to, and had many friends, while he was quiet, matter of fact, frequently moody, and seemed depressed. They began seeing each other after a set-up blind date in February and the decision to marry came about in August. They had two months to organize their wedding. That period and the day of the ceremony still remain in her memory as one of the saddest events of her life.

They both completed their undergraduate studies. Doug earned a degree in electrical engineering two years prior to Nora's BA in French. He was unable to find a job in the same city, and she was hoping to land a teaching position in one of the local high schools that included a study of foreign languages in their curricula. Being unemployed, they had to live with their parents who agreed to pay for their wedding reception. To say the least, the circumstances surrounding that occasion were far from ideal. Furthermore, to make the situation even more challenging to navigate, there was their parents' first meeting. It was obvious that they differed not only in the level of their education – Nora's were high school graduates and Doug's had college degrees – but they also had opposite characters, especially the mothers. Both were opinionated, sharp-tongued, and hard to please. The fathers were quiet and nodded in support of their wives who were making all the decisions regarding the organization of the wedding.

They decided that it should take place in the spacious three-bedroom condo of Nora's future in-laws instead of using a professional wedding venue because it would be much cheaper. The mothers would prepare a buffet dinner, and Nora's parents' friends who owned a pastry shop would donate the wedding cake. Neither she nor Doug were asked for their input in selecting a menu. His brother, Alan, would buy all the beverages. Hosting a reception in the condo meant that the guest list should not exceed thirty, which eliminated Nora's mother's entire family and from her father's side only one cousin was invited. Her childhood girlfriends were excluded. The maid of honor came with her husband. Doug's brother and his family of four were on the list along with his only aunt, his best man with his wife, and a few college friends. His parents also invited two neighbors from the condo above theirs whom Nora didn't even know. She was not surprised that her mother's family as well as her girlfriends were offended by being left out because they expected to take part in the celebration.

Doug and Nora concluded that letting their parents dictate the format and the content of their reception was less stressful than trying to question or alter their decisions. On the other hand, they ignored his family's wish for a church ceremony and opted to be wed by a justice of the peace in a town hall. The selection of the wedding attire also became problematic, as well as the purchase of the wedding rings. Alan, being well-off thanks to his thriving dental practice, gave him money for an appropriate suit for the occasion. Instead of buying it in a store for grooms, Doug bought an everyday herringbone pattern suit in a mall. Nora didn't know that until she saw him at the Town Hall. In the seventies, it was fashionable that brides wore long white gowns and veils or wide brim hats. Nora didn't want to follow suit and asked a local seamstress to sew an above-the-knee, cream-colored sleeveless dress with a matching button-down coat for her. She went to a known cobbler and ordered the same color custom made shoes. Instead of an elaborate, large wedding bouquet, she chose a small one made of wildflowers.

The wedding day arrived quickly. In the morning Nora went to her usual hairdresser to have her shoulder-length brown hair styled. After the woman sprayed her locks generously with hairspray, Nora looked in the mirror and was disappointed with the result. The hairdo didn't suit her, causing her to feel like a different person. It was too late to change it, and she stoically accepted it as she had done with all the other details related to her wedding. The plan was that Doug's best man, Ivan, would pick her up at her parents' apartment and that he would come to the Town Hall separately with his brother and parents. Practicality was that day's motto. At three o'clock sharp Ivan honked from his old Pontiac, inviting Nora to come out. Her parents drove in their equally aged Volkswagen. Before exiting the apartment, she took one last look at herself in the full-length mirror hanging in the narrow, dimly lit hallway. Her dress and coat camouflaged her slightly protruding stomach, the color of the shoes perfectly matched her outfit but were too narrow and already hurting her swollen feet. Her face was joyless and tense as if she were about to face something ominous once she opened the door in front of her. The expression of a happy and excited bride was not hers to own.

"I hope that my bouquet of wildflowers will lift my mood," she thought.

Her maid of honor, Victoria, picked it up at the florist and handed it to her at the entrance to the Town Hall.

Nora didn't remember a word that was said in the car during the thirty-minute drive across the downtown area. She recalled entering a large room full of happy brides in long white gowns and large-rim hats and grooms clad in black suits and ties. They looked like clones, and she was glad to have chosen nontraditional attire. Theirs and their wedding parties' giggling and cracking jokes created a celebratory atmosphere while they waited for their turn to enter another spacious room for the officiation ceremony. Nora's was the third on the schedule. Shortly after her arrival, her parents came in complaining that they had had a tough time parking their car because the Town Hall garage was full. Doug and his family showed up just a few minutes before the clerk invited them in to begin the ceremony. She was embarrassed and annoyed seeing him wearing an inappropriate to the occasion suit because to her it meant that he was not honoring either her or their marriage.

The room they entered had several rows of chairs to accommodate the parents, family members, and friends of the wedding couple. The first row facing the justice of the peace was reserved for the bride and groom and their two witnesses. Nora and Doug sat on the assigned chairs flanked by Ivan and Victoria, while the rest of their wedding party took a seat behind them. The justice was a middle-aged woman dressed in a black robe. She warmly welcomed everyone present and proceeded to recite a Statement of Purpose. Nora remembered her and Doug repeating the wedding vows to each other after her, but she didn't grasp their content, as if a dense fog had enveloped her brain. She snapped out of it when the justice asked her what her last name would be.

"I will keep my maiden name and add my husband's."

Doug had agreed with her choice when they discussed it days earlier, but her father-in-law was stunned as shown on the video of the ceremony that his brother shot. He didn't expect that she would defy tradition by not taking only her husband's last name. Nora's decision was based on her desire to keep part of her ante marriage identity alive and not to disappear into another one brought about by taking the new surname. She had watched that happen to two of her mother's girlfriends. After the friends' divorces, they struggled with the dilemma of whether to continue using their married name or change back to their maiden names. She heard one of them even saying, "I don't know who I am any longer." Those girlfriends remarried and took their second or third husband's last name. Nora wondered if they took on a new identity each time. She didn't want to turn into one of those women hidden behind their husbands' successful careers and well-regarded social status while their own identity ceased to exist because the marriage tradition demanded it.

The rings they exchanged in the following phase of the ceremony had their own story. Doug's father gave him his wedding band because his parents thought that buying a new ring was an unnecessary expense. Doug bought Nora's in the JCPenney's jewelry department. It was a narrow fourteen-carat gold band that fit her small ring finger. He paid for it with the money left over from the purchase of his suit. She wore hers until their fortieth anniversary when Doug surprised her by buying new wedding rings for both of them in a fancy jewelry store. He had lost his first one a month after their wedding by leaving it on the edge of the sink in the bathroom of the cafe where he used to meet Ivan every week. He never put on the new one because he found it uncomfortable on his chubby fingers.

After they exchanged rings and signed the marriage license, the justice of the peace pronounced them husband and wife. They turned toward each other and, a bit hesitantly, kissed as if being embarrassed to do it in front of a large crowd. The room exploded with applause and all present congratulated them. Nora looked at Doug's face and saw the same expression of wonderment that she felt as if they were both launched into unknown waters. It was a short ceremony, and her mother-in-law reminded everyone that the reception in their condo would begin at seven o'clock.

Once all gathered, the wedding party split into two groups – both parents, Doug's brother and his wife, his aunt, and the neighbors sat in the largest room, while young people were in Nora and Doug's future bedroom. The buffet was set up in the formal dining room. Nora didn't remember anymore what the two mothers had prepared. She only recalled the wedding cake with the black figurines of the bride and groom on top. Soon after both groups ate, the older crowd began to drink and sing. They celebrated their wedding in a way that was the most entertaining to them.

Nora never forgot the incident her mother created amid all that gaiety. She heard her voice calling her from the hallway. She found her putting her coat on, ready to leave. She was upset because she had burned a hole in her new green jersey dress with a cigarette. Nora knew that her mother had had too much to drink and failed to notice that hot ashes were falling on her dress. After a while, she was finally able to convince her to stay because it was her only daughter's wedding, and she should stop thinking only about herself. Nora and Doug entered the large room only once to pose in a group photo for posterity.

The young group in the small room talked about plans for their future and joked. The entire condo became enveloped in cigarette smoke that began to bother Nora. Her swollen feet were hurting her even more because she had on her new shoes the entire day. Someone took a photo of Doug holding her on his knees as they both smiled, she shily and looking down while he was grinning. Nora always liked that picture because it radiated with tenderness. Her wedding day was supposed to be the happiest day of her life as most brides describe it; instead, she was overwhelmed with doubts. She asked herself, "What do I do now?" She couldn't turn the clock back. She questioned if Doug would come through for her and reassured her that their future would not be as bleak as their wedding. That day, he was overcome with his own uncertainties - was Nora the right person for him? How are they going to cope when the baby arrives? Would they find jobs?

The wedding party left around eleven o'clock. Doug and Nora, exhausted physically and emotionally, were at last alone. Thinking back on that day, she realized that they blindly entered the institution of marriage because they thought that it was the right thing to do considering they were bringing into the world another person who deserved to grow up in a two-parent family unit. The success of their marriage was even more questionable because neither of them was madly in love, the feeling that usually helps young couples overcome initial marital problems. They "liked each other" was a more accurate description of their relationship.

"What time is it?"

"You slept for two hours. This was not a nap. This is the reason you cannot sleep during the night."

"Is there any hot water in the coffee pot?"

"I just heated some."

Nora watched Doug slowly walk into their kitchen. His worn-out waffle tea shirt was hanging over his bony shoulders and his cotton sweatpants were all stretched out.

"I have to buy you some well-fitting clothes to wear in the house. You look awful."

"Thank you, dear. I love you," he mocked her with a grin.

She felt flooded with love for that man who came through for her, if not on their wedding day, but during their fifty years of marriage.

The Letter

On one late September afternoon Avery sat at the table in a small outdoor neighborhood cafe in Cleaveland sipping her hot latte and listening to her friend Martin describing his life during the Covid pandemic. The sun's rays struggled to penetrate through the still dense oak foliage and warm up her back. She didn't mind cooler temperatures after a scorching summer and hoped that the Indian summer would not circumvent her city that year and force her to meet her friends indoors. She was looking forward to finally getting together with Martin because the last time she had seen him was four years ago shortly before he and his wife moved from Cleaveland to an old, quaint Ohio village where she had inherited a one-story house after her oldest aunt's passing. Being in their late sixties and life-long urbanites, they were ready to relocate away from the city's hustle and bustle. In addition, the two of them had trouble climbing stairs into their bedroom situated on the second floor of their spacious suburban home.

Avery looked at Martin and concluded that he didn't look much different from their high school days. He was recognizable, which was not the case with many of their ex-classmates whose appearances became altered as they aged. His only noticeable physical change was his white hair and beard, both of which used to be red. He was still heavyset, and his thick beard reached his chest. His glasses rested on the bridge of his nose instead of on the indentation on the top of it just as she remembered him wearing them in high school. He had severe myopia since childhood.

"I need bifocals now, and I'm scheduled for cataract surgery in a couple of months," he explained noticing that Avery was about to ask him about his vision.

Avery was surprised to see him ordering Coca-Cola instead of the former usual glass of white wine which confirmed one of their close friend's comments that he had stopped drinking because of several health issues treated with medicines whose efficacy would be hampered if he were to continue to indulge in drinking alcohol.

"So, Martin, how are you? What have you been doing in the last four years?"

"I am so glad to finally be able to meet you! You look the same as in the photo from our high school graduation. I came across it while unpacking one of the moving boxes."

"Come on, not true! I have aged. Can't you see my lined face?"

Avery liked his compliment because it affirmed that her efforts to take care of her health were working. She knew that her deep and fine facial wrinkles were unavoidable as she grew older despite the variety of moisturizers and creams she used. Her body, on the other hand, she successfully kept in shape by attending Pilates classes and swimming in a nearby YMCA. She also walked four or more miles daily year-round.

"I have been extremely busy with writing, translating, and occasionally offering an on-line workshop on the challenges of producing quality translations. My social security doesn't keep pace with inflation, and the extra income I earn from doing those things helps us maintain the standard of living we are accustomed to."

"It's good that you can continue to be productive. Tell me, how is life in the slow lane?"

"I love it, and Martha enjoys tending our small garden. She misses the kids, though, but then we do visit them whenever we have doctors' appointments in town. Just recently, I had problems with my back that my neurologist said were due to my sitting in front of a computer daily for ten hours. Thanks to intensive physical therapy I was able to begin to walk first with crutches, then with a cane, and now I don't need any medical devices anymore. What is going on with you?"

"I have been well and easily weathered through the July Omicron. I had no fever, just a bit of a runny nose and a cough, both symptoms lasted only a couple of days. I am not sure if you remember that I retired six years ago. I had enough after having spent more than forty years in the classroom. I must admit that I don't miss teaching at all. I use my free time to read and write stories, a favorite hobby that I have been doing forever. Four of them even appeared online in different literary magazines. I am also busy helping drive our grandkids when the school buses are not running for a lack of drivers or bad weather. By the way, how are your kids?"

"They both are doing okay. Lana is teaching, has one son, our only grandson, and John is more entrepreneurial. Do you keep in touch with anyone from our high school class?"

"Only with Sandra. We see each other occasionally. She is better informed than I am and told me about seeing the death notices of Stan's, Andrea's, and Matt's passing in the obituary in the paper. We are at an age when it should not surprise us. And you, do you see anyone when you are in town?"

"I usually meet Andy and a couple of other guys from other classes that you probably don't know. I almost forgot to tell you that Will left a letter for you a few years ago. I was supposed to give it to you. Sorry, it must still be somewhere in one of the still unpacked boxes. Our relocation to the village was rushed accompanied by the usual frenzy of deciding what to take with us and what to get rid of. Then, once we moved, we had to adjust to a new house and a new life. You know how that goes."

"Oh, don't worry about it. It most likely has nothing important written in it. Since you mentioned Will, how is he doing? I haven't seen him for years."

"I ran into him in town before Covid hit, but after we exchanged a couple of banal greetings, he began his usual cynical, insinuative, and hard to follow diatribe that I didn't want to hear. He was not interested in a normal conversation between two friends. I was just an ear to him that was supposed to process, according to his beliefs, spouts of his wisdom. I interrupted his soliloquy by telling him I had a doctor's appointment. Frankly, I couldn't stand him. I think that others who had to deal with him on both the professional and private level felt the same way. Because of his bizarre behavior, the Department of Linguistics, where he taught phonetics, forced him into early retirement. I am sure that he is struggling financially."

"You are right. His difficult personality alienated him from everyone. The last time I saw him, he tried to exude a pose of one who knows and understands the world, unlike the rest of us incapable of grasping the true meaning of anything. I found his monologue boring and a cliché."

"I am sorry for cutting our meeting short. I have an appointment in half an hour. I am so happy that we got together. Let us stay connected. Here is my business card with my email address and phone number. I lost your email. Write to me, and I'll save it this time."

As Martin was getting ready to leave, Avery remembered that she promised her next-door neighbor that she would come for a coffee klatch later in the day. He hung his worn-out leather bag over his shoulder, called the waiter, and insisted on paying the bill despite Avery's protest. She stepped away from the small round table, got closer to Martin, and was ready to hug him. She disappeared into his bear hug despite the overall paranoia and the government recommendation to refrain from embracing because Covid was still around. Neither she nor Martin wanted to leave each other saying only a generic "Bye." Their friendship was true and long-standing; thus, a tight squeeze was a fitting end to their meeting.

Slowly walking back home on the wide, paved sidewalk that weaved among the tall oak trees on one side, Will's lost letter was on Avery's mind because it brought back memories of their five-year-long relationship. She felt as if her past had suddenly become unearthed. Her interest in finding out the content of that letter was secondary to the flow of recollections that it brought to the surface. Her memories were no longer painful; they were just a series of images resembling the redacted scenes from a long movie. There was only one memory from her relationship with Will that she considered meaningful – it was their first kiss.

Avery met Will through Martin when both were seniors in high school. Martin used to hang out with professionals connected with theater productions. They included directors, actors, scenographers, costume makers, and among them was Will, who in addition to teaching phonetics also gave private diction lessons to young actors. Martin attended all their performances to learn as much as possible about the elements that constitute a good play because he aspired to become a playwright himself. When he wrote his first short comedy play, he thought that students enrolled in the high school drama class could stage it and present it in the school auditorium at the end of the year. He asked Will if he had some free time to teach the correct dialogue pronunciation to his classmates. Avery was in that class, and Martin assigned her as the female lead. The school's principal agreed to pay Will for his once-a-week work with students.

The first time he entered the classroom, Avery was surprised to see a short, skinny man with dark curly hair and brown piercing eyes that were the most impressive part of his round, clean-shaved face. His miniature stature contrasted with her picture of people connected with theater and film as being tall and handsome. She fashioned her assumption by seeing many movies that featured statuesque male leads. When he spoke, his voice was deep and melodic. He had a quick smile that helped students relax while they tried to follow his suggestions on how to flawlessly pronounce each sentence. He never missed praising them for their efforts. Avery was fascinated by his knowledge of literature and his poise. His natural charm was not lost on her. Being twenty-five years old, he was quite different from her male contemporaries plagued with teenaged insecurities and issues of self-identity. Will was the first young adult man that she had ever met. In the months that followed, she fell madly in love with him. He was her first love. Will became aware of her affection for him and was not indifferent to her feelings. He overlooked her adolescent age and decided to date her.

The first time Will took Avery out was the New Year's Eve celebration of the same year that they had met. He and Martin picked her up at her parents' house who told them that she should return home shortly after midnight. Her mother disliked Will from the very beginning. He offended her by refusing to drink a shot of a domestic brandy that she had offered to him. Without thanking her or inventing an acceptable excuse he simply said, "I only drink Greek cognac." Avery failed to register his rudeness and arrogance at that moment, but those two-character flaws came into full view in the subsequent years of their relationship.

After wishing a Happy New Year to Avery's parents, the three of them walked five blocks to the condominium of their mutual friends who were hosting a party. Martin left before the lights were dimmed and the record player turned off to let the partyers loudly count the last seconds of the Old Year. Will and Avery began to kiss before all the others while exchanging New Year's wishes. She was overtaken by the intensity of her emotions and sat motionless while Will was pressing his lips on hers. He held back from touching any part of Avery's body because he sensed that she was not ready for it. Furthermore, he was aware that she was just a teenager, thus legally off limits. He walked her home holding her hand and philosophizing that her love for him was for a short duration and would pass as fast as the train they watched speeding over tracks on the embankment on their right. She didn't believe him, convinced that her love was everlasting. As she lay in bed that night, she felt the happiest she had ever been. It never crossed her mind to question the sincerity of his feelings for her. People in love tend to cocoon themselves in their bubble of bliss that they safeguard by ignoring reality.

"Strange, how I still so vividly remember that night," Avery mused. "It's good that I kept at least one positive memory of Will because all the rest of them contribute to my conclusion that he was truly a bad man whose disregard for others destroyed his own life, and it would have ruined mine if I had stayed with him."

Before Will, Avery had only a few crushes on the boys from her high school that never progressed beyond exchanges of semi-love notes during recesses. Not having any experience dating, she didn't realize that seeing him once or twice a month was not the norm for a healthy and committed relationship. He used to call her on Saturday mornings to invite her to an early afternoon movie. He would select the film he wanted to see. They were often European pictures dealing with complex socio-political themes that were hard for her to understand. After those two hours of holding hands and an occasional whisper in her ear to explain a particular scene, Will would tell her to go home because he had things to do.

Occasionally Avery would see him downtown in the company of different women, and sometimes it would be the same one. He would pretend not to notice her. She grew jealous and began to ask him who those women were. Will would appease her by saying that they were just colleagues. Their relationship was platonic in the first year but once it turned sexual, he lost interest in her as a person. She became a no-strings-attached commodity to satisfy his libido every three weeks.

They had sex in small, downtown rooms adjacent to others that the owners of the condominiums would rent to different tenants. The rooms all reeked of cigarettes because he chain-smoked Camels. His clothes would hang on metal racks, and his books were scattered over the cheap wall-to-wall carpeting. He always had one or two lemons on a nightstand and a bottle of warm sparkling water that he couldn't ice because there was no free space even for a mini fridge. She guessed that those two items were remedies for his frequent hangovers. Avery thought that they were making love but began to question why she never felt any physical pleasure while doing it. She pondered if something was bodily wrong with her. Years later, she was in a happy and giving relationship that made her realize that Will was an inconsiderate and unimaginative lover who only took care of his own sexual needs. His rhythmical thrashing while lying on top of her had nothing to do with the intimacy of true lovemaking. The absence of ecstasy at the end of it would leave her feeling depleted of all emotions. He objectified her to the point that he no longer had qualms about frequently substituting her with other women. She sensed that he was unfaithful but convinced herself that those affairs would not last and that he would always return to her. He made her lose all her self-respect.

An unforeseeable event that forever altered Avery's life took place when she was a junior in college. During intercourse, Will would use a condom every time primarily not to impregnate her because that would require him to make decisions with far-reaching consequences for both of them. He was in his late twenties, and the most important things to him were his freedom and his vagabond-like behaviors played out through diverse, noncommittal relationships. That fateful Saturday afternoon, he discovered that he had run out of rubbers but decided to have sex with Avery anyway. She didn't mind because she hoped that this novel experience would enable her to finally reach the desired climax. She was wrong. Will did not move the earth under her, nor did he teach her how to help herself achieve it. She was not even disappointed with it because throughout years of a dissatisfying sex life with him she became indifferent to it. However, the result of that Saturday tryst caused her to panic. Her period failed to come on time the following month. She called Will asking him to meet her in one of his favorite cafés. Despite being nervous and terrified, she gathered all her strength to calmly inform him that she might be pregnant. Without missing a beat, he coldly said:

"You cannot have this child. Get rid of it!"

Seeing Avery's bewildered look after hearing his reaction, he softened his command by giving her a reason for his refusal to have the child:

"An ex-girlfriend of mine delivered a mentally damaged boy eight years ago. I was the father. There is something wrong with my chromosomes."

He knew that this revelation would scare any future mother, especially one as young as Avery. The situation at hand was too serious to be taken lightly; thus, she believed that he was telling the truth. He even named the woman to beef up his lie because he was certain that Avery would not take it upon herself to contact her and verify his claim.

While anxiously waiting for her period to come, Averi tried to analyze the state in which she found herself and the consequences that would follow if she made a wrong decision. Her logical thinking was often clouded by an overwhelming fear. On the one hand, she was afraid of her family's reaction when she would tell them about her pregnancy, and, on the other, she feared the procedure itself. She watched her mother walking through the house with an expression on her face that bordered between inquisitive and angry. Avery was aware that she kept track of her periods, especially in the last several years because she rightfully concluded that her daughter was sleeping with Will. Consequently, her mother noticed the absence of her period on the date when it usually would start. She remained, uncharacteristically for her, silent, which convinced Avery that her mother expected her to decide what she was planning to do and then inform her about it.

The looming question of whether to keep the baby or to abort it was complex and forced Avery to approach it in the context of her entire future life. Her wrong choice would be irreversible. She felt all alone in the midst of circumstances that demanded mature, adult resolution. Instead, she was surrounded by those who put aside her needs and defended their own interests – Will, his freedom and her mother, the family's honor that would be ruined if she kept the child. It became clear to her that she must do what was best for her. She realized that as an unwed mother she would have to live with her parents indefinitely because as a teacher she would not earn enough to rent an apartment and hire a babysitter to watch the baby while she worked. Moreover, on a daily basis, she would have to listen to their upbraid regarding her failed relationship with Will.

An additional element and the most important one that factored into Avery's reasoning was Will. She understood that by having his child she would have him forever in her life. It was possible that he would change his mind and would insist on marrying her with the sole purpose of raising the child together. Even if she agreed to marry him, deep down Avery knew that their marriage would not last because Will was unable to change. He would continue with his philandering, would be more absent than present in the house, and would continue to drink heavily. She would not be able to tolerate any of those vices. In summary, of all odds stacked in favor of ending her pregnancy, Avery concluded with a heavy heart that this was what she should do. Prior to reaching her final decision, she also considered adoption but gave up that idea because she knew that once she held the baby in her arms, she would not be able to give it up. As gut wrenching as her first resolve was, the second one felt like a breath of fresh air that she inhaled with lungs wide open. She decided to leave Will for good. It was the best decision of her life.

Thankfully, her period arrived after a delay of one week due to the onset of a cold. When Will called to find out the result of the pregnancy test, she told him that it was negative even though she had never taken it.

"This is great!' he gleefully responded. "There are two good movies playing in theaters. Would you like to go tomorrow? It's our Saturday."

"No. I have an exam and have to study for it. Bye," she rebuffed him and hung up the phone.

Occasionally, he would call her expecting a more cordial reception, which would mean that she was ready to resume their relationship, but she kept those conversations non-committal and brief. Furthermore, those phone calls began to annoy her, especially the seductive tone of his voice that she once considered irresistible. The emotional hurt he had inflicted upon her during those five years of togetherness made her resolute not to ever subject herself to such treatment again, not just from Will, but from any other man she would encounter in the future.

After a while Avery began to date again and met at one of her friends' party an architect, Henry, two years older than her. They began to see each other every other day, went to movies and theaters, and were never short of topics to talk about. He was easy-going, unpretentious, frank, smart, witty, and charming in his own quiet way. He was tall, athletically built, because he trained as a swimmer for his high school team and continued to do it recreationally throughout college. Avery was attracted to him at all levels and sensed that he could be her life-long partner.

The feeling was mutual, and they married after a short courtship. Their wedding was an intimate affair celebrated only with immediate family members and close friends. They bought their first cul-de-sac house with a large, wooded yard where their three boys born in quick succession liked to play. She taught English at a local college and retired at sixty-seven, and Henry was still designing plans for contemporary homes to be built in suburbs across town. Their sons were all grown-up, with families of their own and teenagers that ate them out of the house and home. Life was good.

After a leisure stroll, Avery reached her house, and as she was unlocking the front door, she suddenly remembered, "I should have told Martin not to burden himself looking for Will's letter, and not to feel guilty if he had lost it." She was not interested in the least in its content because she was sure that there was nothing written in it that would change her opinion of Will as being the epitome of a bad person. Moreover, she was certain that he had copied either verses from a known poet or paragraphs from a famous novel because he was incapable of writing anything original since that would require him to honestly evoke his true feelings. Avery's assumption was based on a supposedly original love letter he had sent to her at the beginning of their relationship. A few months later, by accident, she came across a novel whose name she no longer remembered from which Will had plagiarized an entire page where the main protagonist expresses his love to a girl he had recently met.

When Avery entered the family room, she found Henry stretched out on the couch and watching YouTube about building a small boat.

"How was your meeting with Martin? How is his health?" he asked without turning away from the TV and looking at her.

"It was fun. We talked about a variety of things. He seemed healthy. He sent his greetings to you. What do you want to eat for dinner?"

"I don't care. You decide. Come here!" He rose from his horizontal position and tapped his hand on the empty spot next to him.

Avery sat down close to her husband and leaned her head on his shoulder. He turned off the TV, extended his right arm to reach her neck, and gently began to massage it. The tenderness of the moment made her teary-eyed.

"What is it? Why are you crying?" Henry asked in a concerning voice.

"It's nothing. I am just so happy."

Seduction Pronto Lang Style

"Learn another language! Experience other cultures! Become a citizen of the world!"

"Learn another language and meet people from different countries!"

"Learn the language of your ancestors! Discover your heritage!"

"The easy and fast way to learn French is to meet a Frenchman!"

"Octoberfest! Join us! We will teach you how to order a beer in German!"

"Feel like dancing flamenco? No need to go to Spain! Come to Pronto Lang, and we will describe it to you in Spanish!"

"Learn Italian in two weeks! When at the Vatican, you will be able to speak to the Pope!"

"Welcome to Pronto Lang! We will teach you any language you want!"

"Don't worry if you don't have an ear for foreign languages! We'll convince you that you do."

"You will move at a fast pace from beginner to intermediate and advanced courses in two weeks. You will become fluent and will not need us anymore. In case you wish to continue with our services, we can translate for you from any language into one of your choice. We'll provide you with a copy of our translation in any format and media you wish."

"Come to us, we are wonderful!"

Mrs. Simson loved foreign languages. Every fall she would enroll in a different language course at Pronto Lang, a language school nearby her house that offered evening classes. She had a job, a family, and limited free time for herself, thus being able to take those classes made her happy.

"Once a week, two hours, I can do that," she thought.

Learning world languages challenged her because she had to master diverse linguistic skills from pronunciation to understanding, to speaking, and to writing. At the same time, she was excited to broaden her knowledge of other cultures. This experience took her to places that she knew she could never afford to visit. Last fall she decided to learn Italian because an Italian family moved next door. Their last name was Agostino, and Mrs. Simson refused to accept the fact that they were third generation Italian Americans, who didn't even know the basic greetings in Italian such as "good morning" or "see you later." For her, they were Italians.

"I must learn Italian because I am sure that at least one of the Agostino's speaks Italian, and I want to be able to talk to my neighbors. Besides, it is such a beautiful sounding, romantic language. Verdi and Puccini composed the best operas," was her rationale to sign up for a beginner course.

The class was held from 7-9 pm each Thursday. There were fifteen students in the class ranging in age from seventeen to sixty-five years old. The high school kids were all first born Italian Americans, whose parents wanted them to learn Italian to be able to talk to their grandparents in Abruzzi and Calabria whom they had never met but surely would in the future. Their parents worked multiple jobs, spoke in broken English, and were too tired to teach them their native dialect after dinner. Mrs. Simson's other classmates were housewives who preferred Pronto Lang over Thursday Bingo in their church; a math professor who suddenly had the urge to learn something not connected to algebra and geometry; a retired auto mechanic with a last name Settepani who decided that it was about time to learn the correct pronunciation of it. He also hoped that its etymology would lead him to the discovery of a place in Italy from which his grandparents had emigrated a century ago. Mr. Badel, a real estate agent in his late forties, was another of Mrs. Simson's classmates. He wanted to learn Italian because the area that he serviced had a vast Italian population that included recent emigrants from Italy with a limited knowledge of English, thus knowing Italian would help him in his business.

Mrs. Simson was a freelance photographer working for a local newspaper. She was a handsome woman in her late thirties, 5'9" tall and underweight for her height, which made her look fragile. Her brown, round-shaped eyes were the dominant feature on her pale face framed by mahogany dyed shoulder length hair parted on one side. She wore discreet makeup to add color to the plainness of her visage. She preferred to dress in understated outfits as if avoiding being noticed. Her demeanor and appearance somehow contradicted the common assumption that most artists, and she being a photographer, was one of them, walk around clad in provocative clothes. Instead, one could easily imagine her wearing a white apron while making an apple pie or old jeans and a hoody hiding behind sahuaros in the Arizona wilderness while taking pictures of rare birds. She spoke softly and slowly, carefully choosing her words. When she laughed, she muffled its sound by covering her mouth with her right hand to not disturb those around her. Mrs. Simson was one of those people who avoided taking part in any public happening because she preferred her privacy. She strived for anonymity and enjoyed life by being invisible. She was also modest to the point that she seldom showed her own family the newspaper issues that featured her photos. However, this self-protectionism of hers did not preclude her friendliness toward others or being above approach, but people needed to seek her out first.

Mrs. Simson married her high school boyfriend soon after they both graduated from college and adapted quickly to her wifehood and subsequently to her motherhood. She lived an ordinary suburban life, undisturbed and protected from existential problems that afflicted some of her friends and colleagues. Her husband worked as an accountant, and their combined income enabled them to buy a small ranch-style house and two cars and to take week-long vacations visiting national parks. Their three children practiced different sports and went to summer camps. She sailed through life as if pushed by a gentle wind across the sea. She felt fulfilled and at ease with herself.

After the first two weeks of classes, Mr. Badel approached Mrs. Simson during ten minutes of a class break.

"Mrs. Simson, would you mind practicing the conversation in Italian with me because I have a difficult time inventing my sentences during a dialogue? I noticed that your fluency is better than the other people in our class. If you agree, we could meet once a week and talk in Italian. I could use your help."

"What do you mean, Mr. Badel?"

"Mrs. Simson, I also noticed that you have almost perfect pronunciation. My American accent is so strong that even our instructor often doesn't understand what I am saying in Italian. This is a real handicap when I try to converse. If you can spare some time, I'll be grateful to meet you at any place any hour that is convenient for you."

"I am not sure how I can help you. My vocabulary is extremely limited. I am a beginner as are you!"

"We could invent short dialogues with topics of common interest, and search for the vocabulary needed for a basic conversation."

"I am sorry. You better ask somebody else to help you because I honestly don't know more Italian than you do." She was trying to get herself out of Mr. Badel's proposal.

"Don't be modest! You did learn more than I did. Why don't we give it a try? What do you say?" he insisted.

Mrs. Simson looked at her classmate's gentle and honest face and said:

"I guess we can try."

"Which day is good for you?"

She thought for a few seconds about her weekly commitments, and said:

"Next Wednesday early afternoon."

"Great! I'll get out of work a bit earlier and schedule my clients for the morning showing."

"Where are we going to meet?"

"There is a donut shop close to my house. On the south side of Joy Road and West Chicago. Do you know where it is?"

"Yes, see you there at 3:00."

"Perfect, at 3:00 next Wednesday."

In the meantime, Mrs. Simson didn't give much thought to the meeting with Mr. Badel. She wrote the practice dialogue, *fare la conoscenza* (meeting someone) by using the simple vocabulary that she found in her English Italian dictionary. The following Wednesday they met at the donut shop full of noisy teenagers. She handed her typed text to Mr. Badel.

"Buon giorno, signora Simson!" (Good day, Mrs. Simson)

"Buon giorno, Mr. Badel!"

"Come sta Lei?" (How are you?)

"Grazie, bene, e Lei?" (Thank you, I am well, and you?)

"Grazie, anche io sto bene." (Thank you, I am also well)

"Che cosa prendiamo, signora Simson?" (What are we going to take, Mrs. Simson?)

"Per me un caffè. Grazie!" (For me coffee, thank you!)

"Anche io prendo un caffè." (I have coffee as well)

"Signora, che cosa fa oggi?" (What are you doing today?)

"Leggo un giornale." (I read a newspaper.)

"Che cosa fa Lei, signor Badel?" (What do you do Mr. Badel?)

"Io guardo la televisione." (I watch the TV.)

Mr. Badel pulled a sheet of paper out of his briefcase and gave it to Mrs. Simson. She looked puzzled, and he explained:

"This is my contribution to our conversation. I spent the past weekend collecting words from my pocket size dictionary and trying to create a dialogue with them. Please don't laugh at my mistakes. I hope that my sentences make sense. Here it goes:

"*Signora Simson, andiamo a casa mia, è vicino! È più quieto lì.*" (Let's go to my house, it is close by! It's quieter there.)

"*Va bene. Lei vive da solo?*" (Ok. Do you live alone?). She read from the given text.

"*No, io sono sposato. Mia moglie si chiama Meggy.*" (No, I am married. My wife's name is Meggy.)

"*Mio marito si chiama George.*" (My husband's name is George.) She added her husband's name that Mr. Badel didn't know while writing his dialogue.

They stood up ready to leave when she improvised her lines:

"Paghiamo prima il conto!" (Let's first pay the bill!)

"Pago io, signora!" (I'll pay!) He remembered the first-person conjugation of the verb *pagare*.

Mrs. Simson drove behind Mr. Badel's car. They reached his one-story house in ten minutes. He parked his Toyota in the two-car garage and pointed to her to leave her Mazda in the empty spot next to him. Mr. Badel unlocked the front door, and they walked into a small living room. She noticed the gaudy furniture and decorations. The sofa upholstered with loud floral fabric leaned against the wall with a large picture window looking out at a small front yard. Two rocking chairs next to it were covered with mustard-colored worn out velvet. On the opposite wall stood a rustic looking oak dining table. The living room was adjacent to the open kitchen with several of its shelves lined with different size colorful figurines. On one of the counters, she spotted a vase with red artificial flowers. A gray color dominated the walls and the kitschy landscape paintings hanging on them. The light green wall-to-wall carpet added to the overall atmosphere of the space that had not been changed in years. She found it oppressive because it also emanated a moldy odor. In Mr. Badel's house everything was simultaneously in perfect order and in terrible disarray.

"*Dove è sua moglie?*" (Where is your wife?) Mrs. Simson continued to improvise their dialogue.

At her surprise, Mr. Badel without hesitating answered in a correct Italian, "*Visita sua sorella.*" (She is visiting her sister.)

"*Dove ci sediamo?*" (Where do we sit?)

"*Sul sofà. Si accomodi signora!*" (On the sofa. Please, sit down!)

"Another grammatically correct answer and the use of a reflexive verb," she thought.

Mr. Badel sat close to Mrs. Simson. His knees were touching hers, and he stretched his left arm across her shoulders. She remained motionless, puzzled by his intimate gestures.

"*Oh, signora Simson, non posso più, andiamo a letto!*" (I can't stand it anymore, let's go to bed!)

This sentence, pronounced in a strong American accent, sounded to her to be rehearsed many times, but she played along with her part.

"*Perché, signor Badel? Non capisco!*" (Why? I don't understand!)

"Because I have wanted it for a long time, and I cannot translate this in Italian!"

He squeezed her hand and leaned toward her trying to kiss her. His face became red from excitement and his heavy breathing. She turned her head away from his, and calmly continued to speak in Italian:

"*Dove è la camera da letto?*" (Where is the bedroom?)

She didn't know why she asked this question. She felt like she was being pulled into another sphere of reality, unknown to her that this situation was about to uncover a daring side of her that she didn't know she possessed.

"*È a destra del bagno. Andiamo!*" (It's on the right of the bathroom. Let's go!)

"*Questo è sciocco, signor Badel!*" (This is crazy!) were the only words she uttered while slowly walking through a dim, narrow hallway toward the bedroom.

"*No signora, è eccitante!*" (No, it's exciting!)

She entered it first, feeling his hot breath on her neck as if he wanted to make sure that she would not change her mind. He was gently pushing her from behind. The bedroom was small and could accommodate only a regular size bed. She noticed that the sheets were changed recently by someone not used to doing it because they were not properly stretched over the mattress. It must have been Mr. Badel, she concluded. The only light in the room came from two safety nightlights plugged in opposite walls. They illuminated the bed and a framed photograph on the nightstand featuring a happy Badel family: Mr. Badel flanked by two young men smiling broadly and a cute, petite woman whose grin showed her protruding teeth.

"You can put your clothes on this chair," he told her in a soft yet commanding voice.

"*Grazie!*" (Thank you!)

Mrs. Simson stood on one side of the bed facing Mr. Badel across from her. They began to take off their clothes slowly and methodically without looking at each other as if each of them was alone in their own bedroom. Dead silence enveloped the place, interrupted only once by Mr. Badel pulling down the zipper of his pants. He neatly folded his clothes on a stool in front of a closet while Mrs. Simson hung hers on the offered chair making sure that her blouse and skirt would not wrinkle. They both stood naked on the opposite side of the bed. Mr. Badel was the first one to resume their role playing by showing Mrs. Simson each piece of clothing he took off.

"Ecco la cravatta, la camicia, i pantaloni, le mutande, le calze e le scarpe." (Here are my tie, my shirt, my pants, my underwear, my socks, and my shoes.)

She followed his suit:

"Ecco la blusa, il reggiseno, la gonna, le mutandine e le scarpe. Adesso ho freddo." (Here are my blouse, my bra, my skirt, my panties, and my shoes. Now I am cold.)

Mrs. Simson looked at Mr. Badel's face tense from eagerness to possess her. She, on the other hand, was blushing like a newlywed not knowing what she was supposed to do. She felt like she was in the "Twilight Zone" and on the verge of fainting.

"Signora, Lei ha un bel corpo." (You have a beautiful body.)

"Grazie, anche Lei." (Thank you, you do too.)

She was being polite because this was part of her upbringing. Never tell the truth if it hurts somebody's feelings. Mr. Badel was just a few inches taller than her, a stocky build with his chest and legs covered with thick, black hair. She saw him as being too massive for his height. The checkered boxer shorts he showed her made her think how they perfectly matched the totality of the image he projected. The colored briefs below his belly button would destroy it. Looking at his nude body and his flushed face disgusted her. She felt her stomach turning but was uncertain if it signaled vomit coming up or her desire to make love to him despite her feelings of repulsion toward him. People sometimes do things for no good reason because they find themselves in situations that defy all logic, and yet they proceed to act on them as if assessing their own limits of tolerance for the inconceivable.

Mrs. Simson and Mr. Badel simultaneously removed the upper sheet from the bed. They pulled it back up all the way to their chins and lay motionless next to each other wondering who was going to make the first move. It was Mr. Badel. She felt his heavy, furry body rolling on top of her making her disappear under him. He held her head in his hands trying to kiss her on the lips. When she saw his gaping mouth full of yellowing teeth, she turned her face toward the happy family Badel photo. From that point on nothing mattered to her any longer. He tried to animate her by sucking her nipples and sliding down to massage her clitoris, to no avail. She remained unmoved, but Mr. Badel was a practical man, a realtor, who didn't waste his weekend for not getting anything in return. After having written his seduction dialogue in Italian, convinced his wife to spend a day at her sister's, and put clean sheets on the bed, he expected a token of gratitude from Mrs. Simson. Not paying any attention to her facial expression telling him to stop, he pried open her legs and penetrated her. It was not painful intercourse; she even climaxed at the same time he did. Nevertheless, that was the saddest episode of her entire life. To make the whole experience even worse, Mr. Badel quickly jumped out of bed, stretched his arm high above his head as a gesture of his complete satisfaction with himself. Then matter-of-factly he spoke:

"Facciamo il letto!" (Let's make the bed!)

He made sure that his wife wouldn't see that somebody had already been lying in it. They straightened the lower and upper sheet, adjusted pillows on the headboard, and put the chair and the stool in their original place. He quickly began putting his clothes on without looking at Mrs. Simson, who was imitating his rapid movements. Her body and her clothes smelled like Mr. Badel, like decay. On the way out of the bedroom Mr. Badel blew a kiss to his happy family photo. Fully clothed he said with a smile:

"Grazie mille, signora Simson!" (Thanks a lot!)

"Non c'è di che!" (You are welcome!) She tried to keep her composure.

"Oh, I forgot to describe what I was doing five minutes ago. Here it is:

"Mi vesto, mi pettino e ritorno al lavoro." (I am getting dressed, I brush my hair and go back to work).

"Ci vediamo il prossimo mercoledì!" (We'll see each other next Wednesday.) He said it very sure of himself as if he had just sold a million-dollar house and earned a nice commission.

He accompanied her to the door. With her hand on the knob, she turned around and asked him:

"Mr. Badel, come si chiama Lei?" (Mr. Badel, what is your name?)

"Mi chiamo Jack." (My name is Jack.)

"Jack, you are a jackass and a jerk, and I am sorry for not knowing an adequate Italian translation for it," she calmly said and slammed the door on her way out.

About the Author

Romana Capek-Habekovic was born in Zagreb, Croatia, and earned a PhD in Italian literature from the University of Michigan in Ann Arbor, where she taught courses in language, literature, and culture. She has published college-level textbooks, and her scholarly articles on twentieth-century Italian authors have appeared in numerous academic journals. Alongside her academic work, she has continued to write both fiction and non-fiction, with her stories featured in publications such as *New Reader Magazine*, *Passager*, *EveryWriter*, *Fauxmoir*, *The Common Dispatches*, *Litbreak Magazine*, and *Bright Flash Literary Review*. Her short story collection, *To the Point*, is available on Amazon.

www.ingramcontent.com/pod-product-compliance
Lightning Source LLC
Chambersburg PA
CBHW061727070526
44583CB00024B/3039